How to Spot a Liar

A Practical Guide to Speed-Read People,
Decipher Body Language, Detect Deception,
and Get to the Truth

How to Spot a Liar

circumstances is the author responsible for any losses, direct or indirect, which are incurred as a result of the use of information contained within this document, including, but not limited to, — errors, omissions, or inaccuracies.

Table Of Contents

2 FREE Gifts

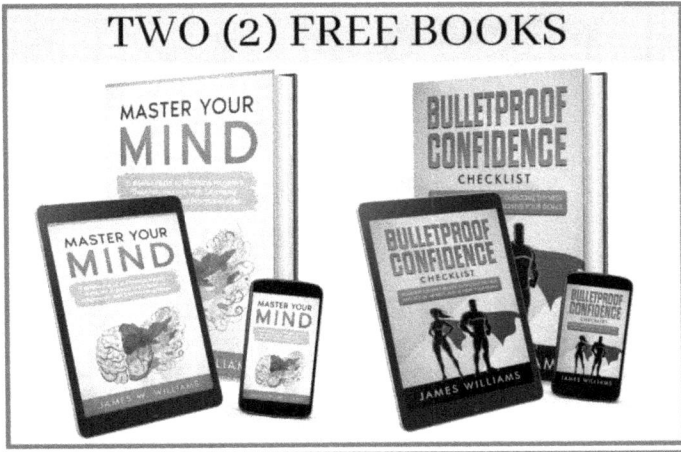

To help you along your personal growth journey, I've created 2 FREE bonus books that will help you master your mind, become more confident, and eliminate intrusive thoughts.

You can get instant access by signing up to my email newsletter below.

On top of the 2 free books, you will also receive weekly tips along with free book giveaways, discounts, and more.

All of these bonuses are 100% free with no strings attached. You don't need to provide any personal information except your email address.

To get your bonus, go to:

https://theartofmastery.com/confidence/

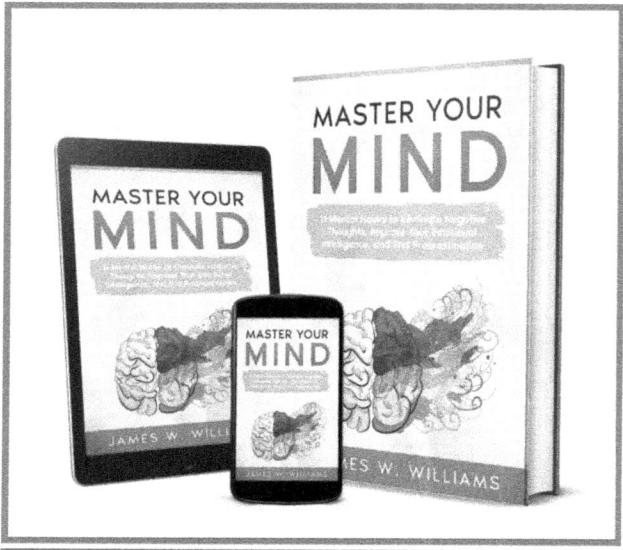

<u>Free Bonus Book #1</u>: *Master Your Mind: 11 Mental Hacks to Eliminate Negative Thoughts, Improve Your Emotional Intelligence, and End Procrastination*

Discover the techniques and strategies backed by scientific and psychological studies that dive into why your mind is preventing you from achieving success in life and how to fix them.

You will learn how to:

- Deal with stress, fear, and anxiety
- Become more emotionally intelligent
- Communicate better in your relationships
- Overcome any and all limiting beliefs you have
- Avoid procrastinating
- Actually enjoy doing difficult tasks
- And so much more!

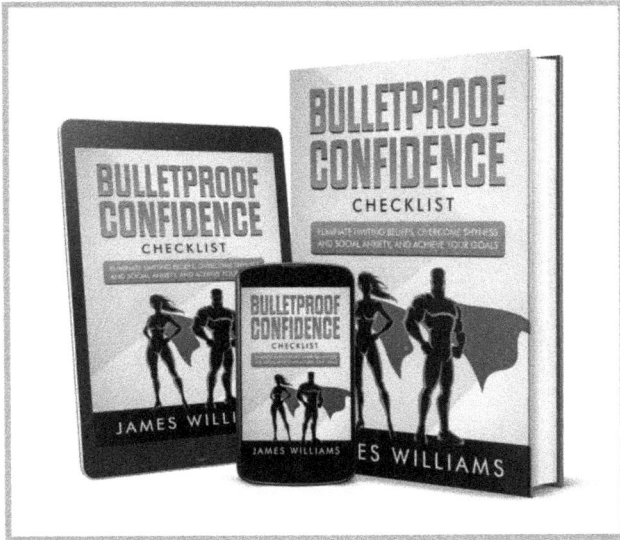

Free Bonus Book #2: *Bulletproof Confidence Checklist: Eliminate Limiting Beliefs, Overcome Shyness and Social Anxiety, and Achieve Your Goals*

In this book you will discover how to overcome the limiting beliefs that results in lack of confidence and social anxiety.

You will learn practical tips to rewire your negative thought patterns, break free from shyness, and become the best version of yourself.

Introduction

"I'm not upset that you lied to me. I'm upset that from now on I can't believe you." - Friedrich Nietzsche

From a young age and at the very start of our childhood, everybody learns that one of the greatest virtues we can have as a human being is to be honest, live honestly, be truthful, and not tell lies. We're told to own up and take responsibility for our actions and the things we say and to be honest with those around us. We're told to tell the truth, the whole truth, and nothing but the truth, and convinced that lying can get us into very deep trouble with our friends, families, and communities.

Yet, paradoxically, we're lied to and tell other people lies constantly. Even though your parents would say to you that lying is wrong (at least they would if they were decent parents), they would still have lied to you all the time. Going back to your very earliest childhood years, you were probably told stories about the existence of Santa and the Tooth Fairy. While this kind of lie may seem somewhat harmless, you were perhaps lied to about where your pets go when they pass away, the shocking things that would happen if you didn't eat your vegetables, and where you'd end up in life if you didn't try your hardest at school.

It's funny because even while humans are this young and were told lies of this context, even young children can still sense the difference between the truth and a lie. We have a gut instinct when something is wrong. This is why children will argue with their parents. They're simply testing out and exercising their ability to tell right from wrong. They will also start to push their boundaries and tell more lies themselves.

Studies show that kids as young as three years old will lie to their parents to get away with certain things. One popular study had researchers place kids in a room with a new, expensive toy which the children were then told not to look at. Of course, being curious kids, they had to take a peek the moment the researchers left the room. When they returned and asked the kids whether they had looked or not, the children would lie through their teeth.

As a bit of an interesting tangent, kids are really good at lying, probably more so than you'd believe. In a 2017 study published by the *Journal of Law and Human Behavior,* "Detecting Deception in Children: A Meta-Analysis," adults were only able to tell when children were lying about 54% of the time. So basically, as close to a 50/50 guess as you can get. The truth is only found out because kids are more prone to leaking telling information later on in the conversation that gives the game away.

As we grow up, we gain more awareness, become smarter, and obtain more emotional intelligence, which means we can lie more. Our lies become more convincing and trustworthy. We know more about how to make it seem as though we're telling the truth and covering our tracks along the way. Of course, this doesn't apply to everyone, and most people grow out of lying, or so you would hope.

The reality is a little different.

Sadly, the present world is full of dishonesty, even more so now than ever before, especially with the current state of politics, social media, and mainstream news media. Constant information from instant sources has created a world where everyone is seemingly confused, nobody really knows what's going on at the heart of most issues, and we're all left feeling a little anxious, a little scared, and not really sure what's happening with anything.

Even in our own relationships, statistics clearly state we're lying to our friends, families, and partners more than ever before.

So, what if I told you there was a way to see through the gaps?

What if there was a way to teach yourself the necessary and essential skills that would enable you to know when someone is lying instantly? It wouldn't matter where you are, what you're doing, or who you're speaking with. You'd have the capabilities to pick up on the signs and know that the truth is being fogged over by other narratives.

A powerful skill? Of course. One you can learn yourself? Absolutely.

Throughout the following chapters of this book, we're going to dive deep into the ins and outs of lying and honesty. We'll be taking a detailed look into where we're at as a society and what the psychological ideas and statistics are towards lying. We'll also figure out the core reasons why we humans lie to each other in the first place.

With this as our foundation of knowledge, we'll then journey into the skills you need to help you figure out whether someone is lying to you in any situation. This is a powerful skill to have on your belt because you'll be able to find out the truth in so many areas of your life. This could be in your family life, at work, in your relationships, with friends, or even while watching the news.

It all starts here, so let's get this show on the road.

Chapter One - Fake News. False Narratives. Who Knows What's Right or Wrong?

"A lie can travel halfway around the world while the truth is putting on its shoes." - Charles Spurgeon

Continuing on from the Introduction, I was amazed to come to the realization that lying is literally everywhere. The more I thought about it, which is all I've been doing for the last few months in preparation for this book, the more I couldn't believe just how commonplace the act of lying is. It all started when I went to dinner with a friend.

I used to go to college with Sam, and we've been friends for years. While close, we both have our own lives, our own families, and so on, so we're busy, but we catch up from time to time a couple of times a year. We met up during the summer and walked around a nearby nature spot all afternoon, talking about everything we'd been up to and righting the world.

We got back to his house and his wife, Sarah, started making dinner while we sat on the deck. His kids came outside and sat down at the end of the garden. They looked very suspicious hunched over behind a large Organization, so my friend called out for them to come over. It turns out they had stolen some candy from a kitchen drawer and were trying to be sneaky in eating it.

"Come on, girls," my friend said. "You've got dinner soon. You know you shouldn't be eating candy."

"But Mom said we could have it," the girls insisted.

Instantly, both me and my friend looked at each other and knew the kids were lying. There's no way Sarah would let them eat candy before dinner, and the fact we'd all been together all afternoon means we already knew that hadn't happened. We laughed, and the kids said they wouldn't eat any more.

At dinnertime, we were eating, and everything was great, but as we got to the end, the kids had barely eaten any of the vegetables.

"Aren't you hungry, girls?" Sarah asked.

The two girls shook their heads.

"Well, whyever not? Have you eaten anything since lunch?"

Of course, Sarah was asking while already knowing they had eaten candy before dinner, specifically with her supposed permission, but they shook their heads again. They straight-up lied to save themselves while guided by the idea that eating candy before dinner was really bad, and they didn't want to be told off or punished for their actions.

Fast forward a few months, and this concept of lying had been playing on my mind a lot. I was at work one day, and we were chatting over drinks at the end of a long week. This was before Trump had been elected as President, but the country was very much in the buildup as being one of the most important elections in modern history. Everyone was talking about politics, and everyone had a lot to say on various subjects.

Sat in a downtown bar, we discussed specific news topics we'd been reading or watching and having a reasonably lighthearted conversation about it all. This was when one of the guys started talking about immigration policy.

He specifically made the point that 25% of the US population was made up of illegal immigrants. His point was that they were in this country, taking up and using valuable resources and straining the national services that proper, "real" US citizens should have first access. You know the drill.

We questioned him, asking where he got that statistic from. Twenty-five percent felt far too high, but he insisted he had seen that figure displayed on the news the previous night. We took out our phones, searched the latest stats, and discovered a figure more around the

4.7% mark, which seemed about right. Yet, even with the stats in front of us, he kept saying he was right. However, at this point in my life, I already knew some of the skills you're going to learn throughout this book on how to detect a liar, and he was ticking a lot of boxes.

As a side note, while editing this book, I've just come back from a break where I was scrolling through Instagram and came across a post shared by an influencer with over two million followers and received a lot of attention. It described how the term "How to hit a woman so no one knows" had been searched 143 million times over the last year.

That's practically impossible (bear in mind the population of the UK is around 60 million, so double that and more), and while the topic of domestic abuse is serious and a real problem, this is a prime example of people using false data and sharing it so willingly and blatantly. At the time of writing, the post and connected articles are being edited to reflect the truth.

So, why am I telling you these stories?

These are just three examples of lies that happen all the time in our everyday lives, and these are lies that are affecting you and the way you live your life. Did you know a new survey released by the World Health Organization shockingly details that over 65% of all meat products in the US contain traces of disease that only exist as a side effect of battery farming?

That's a lie. I just made that up. Whether you trusted it because it sounded like it could be right, or because it was printed in a book, or even if you doubted it from the beginning, putting thoughts like this into your head makes you think and act a certain way. How could you not? After all, your mind is designed to soak up information, then process that information. Your mind then uses data to try to make the right decisions to help you live your life to the best possible version it can be.

When you think of living your life in this way, the information you're using to make your day-to-day decisions must be correct and as accurate as possible.

The Facts about Lying

Let's take a look at the actual statistics surrounding the concept of lying. Psychological research shows that the ideas of lying come to us from a very young age; at least 90% of children by the age of four have started to tell lies. That we already know, which makes sense as a concept.

The very act of growing up is about testing boundaries and figuring out what works and what doesn't. Imagine a very stereotypical child in a situation where they've drawn all over the walls. Their parents confront them and ask if they did it. They cry and nod their head and get told off for defacing the house. Next time something like this happens, the parents ask whether the child did something wrong and, scared of being told off and punished, they say they didn't.

Of course, in a situation like this, the child will clearly get found out because there's literally no way the drawing on the walls could have happened. Sometimes it's super obvious that the child has done something wrong, but there will be other times where they'll get away with it. Think about if there's a sibling involved that can be blamed, or it's a lie about eating a biscuit that is questioned once and then never mentioned again. Remember, an adult can only accurately work out if a child is lying around 54% of the time. If the child gets away with their lie, this confirms that the process of lying has worked. This sadly helps to form the pattern in their brain that will make them far more likely to lie in the future.

In most cases, most human beings will end up with a brain pattern that says lying is wrong and we shouldn't lie about a lot of serious things. However, at the same time, we accept we can lie about minor things, known as little white lies. Depending on the situation, these lies could include not wanting to hurt someone's feelings or hiding the fact you're taking a friend to their surprise birthday party. Whether it's right or wrong to lie in such a situation is subjective, but it's a belief that many of us hold.

Some people will have different experiences and will lie all the way through their lives as compulsive liars because the process of lying seemed to work consistently from a young age. Being able to spot and recognize these people is so important in your life, so you know who you're dealing with and deciding who you want to have relationships with.

However, statistics show that lies are perhaps far more commonplace than you may think. Data shows that the average adult cannot get through a simple ten-minute conversation without lying once, and averagely will tell about three lies during this time.

This goes much further, with stats like:

- 80% of women state they will often tell "harmless" lies

- 13% of people lie to their doctors

- 70% of liars say they would tell the same lies again

- Liars believe that around 1 in 7 lies are discovered

- Men lie to their partners, bosses, or colleagues about six times a day

- 30% of people lie about their exercise and diet routines

- Around 10% of lies are exaggerations of the truth

- Approximately 60% of lies are outright and blatantly false and contain no truth whatsoever

To put this into perspective, if the average person, either male or female, of any age, lies around four times per day, this equals an incredible 1,460 lies per year, and since this is the average of what every single person is doing day in and day out, that's a lot of dishonesty to keep your eyes open for and to decipher for yourself.

The point is, having skills to identify these lies is paramount if you want control of your life. You need to spot these lies so you can instead find out the truth of a situation. Here's an example to wet your whistle.

You're working on a project at work, and you're talking to someone on your team. They tell you they're working on the presentation and it's going to be done by the end of the week. Using your powers of deduction, you figure out their lies and that they are simply procrastinating instead of holding the hope that they'll get it done later in the week. However, you know it's probably just going to be rushed out the night before.

You detect the lie and probe deeper to find out this is the truth. You tell the person that they're not suited for this project because they're not taking it seriously, assigning them a different role, and giving the presentation to someone more suitable. The work is completed to a high standard, and the project is a success. The person you spoke to initially realizes they don't want to be the procrastinating person anymore and sets forward to be better.

It's a win-win for everyone involved. This is a far better outcome than receiving the project presentation after the deadline, the quality not being good enough, the project failing because the client isn't happy, and then all the consequential problems stemming from this situation. It's all avoidable by possessing the skills to spot a lie.

So, let's start detailing how you can spot them. Before we jump into the skills themselves, we're going to take a trip into the psychology of lying. This is vital because it will build up your understanding of why people lie in the first place and the thought process behind lying, enabling you even more of a foundation on how to spot liars and what situations you could be in that will make someone want to lie in the first place.

Chapter Two - Why People Lie

"Liars are the cause of all the sins and crimes in the world." - Epictetus

There are endless reasons why people could tell a lie. Some of these reasons are obvious, such as the reasons for the kids lying to their parents because they want to avoid getting into trouble or someone lying about political statistics because they want people to think they're educated. Maybe someone wants to push their narratives and beliefs onto other people using false information (which is shockingly more common than you may think, especially with the current condition of the world's media).

On the other hand, some lies may not be as obvious, and some lies you may figure out and be left wondering why that person even lied in the first place. In this chapter, we're going to look at some of the core motives behind lying, enabling you to become aware of situations where lies may be taking place. It's in these situations you can apply your new skills of lie detection with extra awareness, thus giving you more chances of figuring out the truth.

So why do people lie?

Again, there are endless reasons, many of which are situation-dependent, but there are typically nine core motives that inspire lies in people, which are as follows:

- To avoid punishment or consequence of an action

- To be rewarded for something

- To protect someone else from punishment or consequence

- To protect themselves from a threat (physical or emotional)

- To impress or gain admiration from others

- To prevent the current pressures of a situation, such as avoiding an awkward meeting

- To exercise power or control over others using information

- To secure someone's privacy

These motives pretty much identify the core and most common reasons as to why someone would lie. If your partner is cheating on you and doesn't want to be found out, they're protecting themselves from the consequence of their action. If a lot of people weren't invited to a wedding, they might have been told the cost of the wedding was just far too expensive to cater for everyone, when really they just didn't want some members of the family there, thus protecting their privacy.

You may say you're running late for a train if you want to avoid an awkward conversation with someone you've just bumped into on the street. You may lie about something you've achieved in your life because you want someone to think you're a better, more capable person than you may be.

Remember, an exaggeration of the truth is still technically a lie.

Judging the Severity of a Lie

While many of the lies you'll tell and will be told can be tiny, the consequence of the lie seemingly minimal, this may not always be the case.

For example, your partner may ask if you've taken the trash out, and you haven't but say you have just so you can get them off your back while you finish your movie or TV show. After the show is finished, you take the trash out, and your partner is none the wiser. Everything seems fine.

This is why it's important to think about the lasting severity of a lie.

You can figure out the severity, and therefore the impact of the lie, by asking three questions:

- How much damage does the lie create?

- How long will the effects of the lie last?

- How is the relationship of the involved people affected by the lie?

Using the same example of taking out the trash, the effect of the lie is relatively harmless since anyone can take out the garbage, and it's not really that big a deal. Even if the trash needs to be taken out to be collected and this collection is missed, it can be annoying, but it can always get picked up next time. It's not the end of the world.

The conclusive effect of the lie is also fairly minimal. The TV show has 20 minutes left, and then the person will take the trash out. The lie lasts 20 minutes, which on the grand scale of things is really not that long.

However, taking the last point into account, how is the relationship of the couple affected? Well, this can happen in several ways. If caught, even over something so small, one partner will feel lied to by the other. This dramatically erodes the trust in the relationship over time, even over something so seemingly small to begin with.

What's more, getting away with the lie in this instance opens the gate for the lying partner to lie more in the future because hey, it worked, so why not? The more success telling lies has, the more elaborate and consequential the lies will become. This is a very slippery slope that can lead to an accumulation of lies that can end most explosively.

This can cause a lot of hurt and pain to everyone involved, and it's not a situation anyone wants to be in. Of course, there's a solid argument that the person shouldn't have lied in the first place, which is a reason why you should never lie in the first place. Even little white lies since they can lead into much darker places, but also why you should be able to spot lies in the first place.

Let's say you're dating someone, and you're getting to know them. You have dates and get closer and start living together and tell them to take the trash out, just like in the example. You ask them if they've done it, and they lie to you. If you don't notice it and never find out, then the lies become more elaborate, and you'll end up in a miserable relationship with zero trust and no connection. Again, painful for everyone involved.

On the other hand, if you have the skills in this book to spot lies, you can instantly identify this person has lied.

This will help you do one of two things. You'll know to create the boundaries that lying is not acceptable in your relationship, thus telling the other person that they must be honest, promoting a trusting relationship. Alternatively, you'll be able to know that your partner is untrustworthy and the relationship is not going to work. This allows you to decide whether you want to stay or find someone else you can actually trust.

Of course, there are times when lying could be deemed as being okay.

Let's say you're organizing a surprise birthday party for a friend and pick them up to take them to the party location. You say this, but you're actually taking them to their surprise party. Using the terms of severity:

- The damage is minimal because you're actually taking them to a party with the people they love

- The duration of the lie only lasts up until the time they reach the party

- Your relationship is actually improved with the lie because the person feels special on their special day

You can always use these three criteria to determine how bad a lie is, whether you're telling one or being told one.

However, I just thought that was interesting knowledge to share. The most important thing to take away from this chapter is remembering the motives behind lying so you can spot them with ease.

Whenever you're in a situation with someone and use any of the skills we talk about in the following chapters and determine someone is lying to you, you can remind yourself of these motives and figure out why someone is lying to you. In the project example we spoke about before, the team member who told you they were working on the presentation when they actually weren't was trying to make themselves look good by not appearing lazy in your eyes. They wanted to make it seem as though they were busy and in control when they actually weren't.

These are clear enough motives for lying. The severity of such a lie can be extremely damaging over the long term. By being able to figure this out, you're proactively avoiding the future problems that could come up as a result of the lie and putting yourself in a much better position and future situation.

Of course, this logic applies to every area of your life, which is why the following skills can be so beneficial. That nicely concludes this chapter, meaning it's time for us to really start focusing on the necessary and essential skills you need to know when it comes to spotting a lie.

The following chapters will contain real, actionable advice that you can start putting into practice right now, so let's begin with the leading and most important signs you'll be able to read in other people, which is, of course, body language.

Chapter Three – Show, Don't Tell: Reading the Physical Signs of a Lie

"There are four ways, and only four ways, in which we have contact with the world. We are evaluated and classified by these four contacts: what we do, how we look, what we say, and how we say it." - Dale Carnegie

It doesn't matter what kind of communication you're talking about; body language is always going to be a core part of understanding the messages and signs that other people are sending you. Someone could say something like, "Yes, you're amazing, and I love everything you do for me," but if they're standing there with their arms crossed while glaring at you, then this statement means something completely different.

While body language is an extensive topic, I'm going to narrow down what you need to know and keep your eyes open for when it comes to spotting a liar. This is usually the most straightforward way you'll spot someone lying, and it's an effective technique to read both people you know really well and even complete strangers. Let's get straight into it.

Look for Inconsistencies

If you know someone quite well, you'll become accustomed to their body language. In other words, the way they hold themselves, stand, walk, sit, and so on. You know what their comfort positions are and what kind of nuances they have in their day-to-day life. This makes it very easy to spot when they're lying to you.

Now, you may not consciously be aware of someone and their body language, but your subconscious mind is. This is why when you're paying attention to someone—and I mean *actual* attention—you know when something is up with them. You have a gut feeling that someone is wrong.

I recently visited my partner's parents and have spent a considerable amount of time with them over the years. We went out for lunch, and we got onto the topic of old pets. My partner talked about a dog they all used to live with when she and her sister were younger. Her father shared how the pup became ill one day and had to be taken to "the farm," or so they were told at the time, later understanding that it had been put down.

However, as we ate and spoke, I noticed both her mother and father looking a little uncomfortable. My partner, seemingly unaware, continued talking about the farm as a funny thing to tell kids when describing death and the nuances with that topic, but something didn't seem right.

Her parents were tense and weren't making eye contact (more on that later), and her mother specifically seemed very stressed out. I nudged my partner, and we spoke about it some more, and it turns out that the dog getting ill had been a lie. In fact, the dog had died after the mother had hit it with the car pulling into the driveway and hadn't seen it run out to say hello. It's a somber story but a great example of a lie that they had told to their daughters that had lasted decades.

This lie was detected because of the change in the consistency of her parents' body language. It had been my partner's father who told the story of the dog being put down, thus telling a lie, and this was evident by the way his body language changed. I couldn't quite put my finger on what, but my subconscious mind noticed the change, as it did with her mother, who clearly also knew a lie was being told.

How can you bring this degree of insight into your own relationships and interactions? Simple.

Listen to your gut.

Of course, I know what you're thinking. It's hard to trust your gut. How do you know when it's right or wrong? How do you know what it's saying? I get it. I lived with social anxiety for pretty much my entire teenage and young adult life. It's hard to zone in and trust that instinct, but it's always taking time to consider it. This is how CIA interrogators and detectives are so good at what they do. They're able to trust their inner judgment.

Your gut instinct is a powerful tool of your subconscious mind and tells you a lot about everything. Learn to trust its judgment. If you're around someone and something tells you that you're being lied to by the person you're speaking with, then the chances are you probably are, so be sure to increase your awareness of what is happening and what is being said to you.

Additionally, you can just look for inconsistencies. For example, most people will make gestures in conversation, like pointing or elaborating a point using their dominant hand. Still, if you're conversing and suddenly they start using their non-dominant hand, this can be a clear sign that someone is being deceptive.

Of course, looking for inconsistencies depends on how well you know the person. It doesn't guarantee that someone is lying to you, so use this as a benchmark to pay closer attention.

If you notice an inconsistency, use this as a sign to apply more focus to the conversation, therefore looking out for other potential signs they're lying. However, being able to trust your gut instinct will take some time and potentially years of practice. While you work on it, here are some other important, more instantaneous techniques you can use to read other people's body language.

Check Out Their Eye Contact

You'll have certainly heard about eye contact being one of the most important signs and indications of body language there is, so I'll make this quick. Some key eye contact signs to keep an eye open for (no pun intended) while conversing with someone include:

- **The duration of eye contact**

Prolonged eye contact for an extended period of time is not an ordinary body language sign, and neither is no eye contact at all. Someone avoiding eye contact altogether is a common sign that they are lying because it's their unconscious mind trying to prevent you from figuring them out. People are typically unable to make eye contact when they feel uncomfortable, and they can feel uncomfortable because they're lying.

An example of this would be a child lying to their parents, and they don't look their parents in the eyes because they don't want to be caught. Instead, they'll look at the floor or their hands. These are prominent giveaways if you know to look for them.

- **Rapid eye movement**

On the same tangent of thought, if someone is looking rapidly around the room, this can be a sign they're lying. This is a sign the unconscious mind is feeling trapped in the current situation because avoiding the truth and telling a lie makes them feel uncomfortable within the conversation. Their darting eyes are a reflection that they're looking for a way out and want to leave.

Imagine you're talking to someone, and you approach a topic of conversation they don't want to talk about, perhaps something like, "Why didn't you come into work last week? They said you were ill. Are you feeling better?" Since the person lied about being sick to get off work, they instantly start looking around with darting eyes because they want to escape since they're forced to lie again to maintain the original lie.

- **Fast, rapid blinking**

Another sign someone could be lying is if they start rapidly blinking—faster than usual, at least. Can you see them begin blinking fast out of the blue when they weren't blinking fast beforehand? Bear in mind that men tend to blink more times per minute than women do anyway, so don't let that cloud your judgment.

Of course, there are many reasons why this could happen, such as getting something in their eye or having a dry eye (perhaps after looking at a screen for an extended period of time), but blinking rapidly is a typical sign that the person is under stress, which can be caused by lying.

- **Direction of gaze**

This is a technique that some interrogators and detectives use when interviewing suspects to see if they're lying. It may take some practice and training to get the hang of it, but it can be a powerful skill if you can master it. The direction of someone's gaze can be a sign they're lying. Typically, most people gaze in the direction of their dominant hand just naturally.

Even as I write this and when I found out about it several years ago after watching a masterclass, even when I'm thinking about what to write next, I find myself gazing to my right side, since my right hand is my dominant one.

Even taking a break from looking at my computer screen, I end up gazing to my right.

This is a natural response that many people have and will do unconsciously. Like the rest of the tips above, if you notice someone gazing to their non-dominant side, this can be a sign that they're lying to you.

Faking a Smile

Perhaps one of the most common body language signs that someone is lying to you is forcing a smile. Many people will have some kind of fake smile when they lie, which happens unconsciously because it supposedly makes the lie more believable. A smile is saying something like, "Hey, see, everything is okay, and I'm telling you the truth. We are friends here that can be trusted."

Of course, if you're able to spot the fake smiles and tell them apart from the real ones, this is a great way to determine whether someone is lying to you. Fortunately, this is much easier than you may first think. When people smile genuinely, it will almost always cause wrinkles to form on their faces, especially around the eyes. A person's nose will also tend to scrunch up.

Practice yourself, and you'll see the difference between a real and fake smile. This technique of reading body language works really well if you already know the person quite well and know what their genuine smile looks like, allowing you to easily spot the fake.

Look for Touching

It's quite a common practice that people will touch their faces when they're lying, and it is especially the case when someone isn't the sort of person to touch their face when they're usually talking. This degree of touching could happen in several ways, whether they're scratching their hair, rubbing their skin, or rubbing their eyes (another way people avoid making eye contact).

Fidgeting and Uncomfortable Actions

This is the most common body language sign that someone is lying that you should be keeping your eyes open for. Fidgeting is a very common sign that someone is uncomfortable (which commonly happens when someone tells a lie) and usually occurs because someone is trying to release or at least process the stress they feel from this lack of comfort.

Fidgeting can manifest itself in lots of different ways, so make sure you're keeping your eyes open for clues. Let's dive into each point for clarity.

Human Behavior or Movement	What's Happening?
Jerky movements (change of positioning)	Dr. Lillian Glass, a behavioral analyst and the author of the book *The Body Language of Liars,* writes, "The head will be retracted or jerked back, bowed down, or cocked or tilted to the side." Basically, if you see someone making a sudden movement with their body, usually their head in a jerky fashion, especially when it happens after being asked a direct question, this can

	be a sign that they are going to lie to what you've just asked.
Fidgeting	When someone lies, they get stressed. That's just the science of lying. The person's heart rate increases as they prepare for whether or not they're going to be found out, and this excess energy needs to go somewhere.

As Mike Vigil, an ex-DEA agent and author of *Deal*, writes, fidgeting is one of the classic warning signs that something terrible is about to happen. When you see fidgeting, it's time to pay extra attention to what is going on.

Again, it all comes down to this buildup of energy that makes people unable |

	to sit still and needs to be vented, all stemming from something, whether that's being dishonest or you're heading into an uncomfortable situation.
Fingernail biting	The trait of nail-biting is only widespread with people who used to do it as a child and continued through into adult life. There are many reasons why this can happen. It can be a sign of boredom or impatience, or even when concentrating really hard as a child. However, it's still, by far, the most common reason and unconscious way of dealing with stress and anxious feelings. This is why it happens when

	someone is lying.
Pulling on lips or ears	This is an unconscious tick that can appear when dealing with stressful, anxious feelings that arise when under pressure, such as when lying. The person may also bite or chew on their lips.
Playing with their hands	Another form of fidgeting. When someone's playing with their hands, it's a sign they are trying to deal with pent-up emotions that need releasing. This is commonplace when someone is lying.
A change in breathing	I've spoken about how when someone lies, the body physically reacts. This is how lie detectors

	work because they pick up on the small changes (usually increases) in the person's heart rate. This is also reflected in the person's breathing, making it a great sign to look out for. You may notice the person starts to breathe faster, or they may stop breathing altogether for a second or two. You may see them take a deep breath or sigh as they process the information they're giving. These are all powerful signs to look out for.
The person begins to sweat (perspiration)	Looking for sweat on the upper lip or forehead is a great way to tell if they're lying or have been lying because it's a sign they

	can't really control.
	The chances are you've seen an exaggerated version of this sign appear to happen to characters in movies as they get nervous and don't want the truth to be found out. Biologically, this is happening because the person's internal anatomy is working overtime to try and keep them looking calm and normal.
Covering of vulnerable body areas	When someone lies or feels anxious in any way, it's a basic human instinct to cover the vulnerable parts of their body. If you've ever had a panic attack, this is because your physical body's fight-or-flight system is

	kicking in. Back in the day when this nervous system was used to save your life, your instinct was to cover the most vulnerable parts of your body to try and keep you alive. We haven't really evolved too much since then. This is why when liars get the spike of nervousness and anxiety, they will naturally feel drawn to cover these vulnerable parts. Such areas will include places like the chest, the neck and throat, the head, and the person's abdomen.
Shuffling feet	All the pent-up extra energy created from the slight adrenaline boost that comes from lying needs to be expelled from

	the body one way or another. A common way this happens is when someone is shuffling their feet around. Shuffling of the feet shows someone is uncomfortable and nervous in the situation and is common when lying. It can even show that the person is thinking about walking away or trying to get away from what is happening and being said.
Covering of the mouth	Just like covering vulnerable parts of your body while lying, some people will also cover their mouth. This is literally the instinctual action someone will do when they want to hide

	the truth and don't want to answer a question nor talk about the subject that's being spoken about. This physical act is the definition of someone trying to stop themselves from communicating. It could be a sign they don't want to talk, or they're about to tell a lie, and they're actively stopping themselves from telling the truth.
Losing the ability to speak	Take a moment to remember famous movie scenes or television shows that depict someone being interviewed by police. As the police get closer to the truth, you see the person being interviewed slowly

	become more and more unable to speak.
	It's as though they try to say something but can't find the words. This sign usually contains a mixture of signs, like an increase in breathing and sweating, because they're trying and failing to figure out how to move forward in the conversation.
	Look for this sign, and you know that the person is either about to lie, has lied, or is trying to figure out whether they want to tell you the truth or not.

It's important to note that the signs of fidgeting when uncomfortable can vary from person to person, so you'll need to think about what the baseline is for the person you're speaking to. However, regardless of the individual sign, they're all reasonably easy to spot as long as you're paying attention to them.

The more you get to know someone, the more in-tune you'll become to their fidgeting actions, and the more accurately you'll be able to detect them happening.

Remember, fidgeting or any of the small actions I listed in the table above will tend to happen when the other person is feeling uncomfortable, not just when they're lying, so use this sign as an indicator to pay attention, not as final proof.

Body Language That Doesn't Match (Mirroring)

One of the most powerful ways to improve your communication with someone is to repeat back the body language movements you see the other person doing. This is known as mirroring and is a way to improve the connection between two people.

You'll have typically seen a dramatized version of mirroring in movies (or you will now that I've mentioned it). It will happen in a conversation when two people are talking, and one person will lean in closer to the other or will rest their head in their hand. The other person will usually consciously or unconsciously mimic the body language.

As Chris Voss, a former FBI negotiator, describes in his book, *Never Split the Difference,* mirroring body language and noticing it in other people is one of the oldest and most tried-and-tested "mind tricks" in the hostage negotiator handbook.

Think about this in your own relationships.

If you're having an intense conversation with someone and they sit back in a relaxed fashion, you're naturally inclined to copy this behavior. Copying body language like this is a human way of showing your connection and compassion to the other person and shows you're empathizing with them. You're connected to one another.

On the other hand, and in the context of this book, if someone is telling a lie, then clearly, the two people are not connected, and there's resistance in the conversation. It's a dishonest and disingenuous interaction. This means there will be a lack of mirrored body language.

If you're talking to someone and you suspect they're lying to you, try adjusting your body language by doing something small, like putting your head in your hand or rearranging how you're sitting. If the other person doesn't follow suit, this could indicate they're lying to you.

Look for Opposites

Sometimes, someone's body language when they're lying won't align with the verbal messages they're sharing, which is especially common with liars who feel under pressure. In other words, when you put someone on the spot, and they haven't had time to prepare their lie in detail, nor rehearse what they're going to say, they're much more likely to give you clear signs they're being dishonest.

For example, if you ask someone what they thought of your presentation just out of the blue and they replied, "I really liked what you said. Yes, it was good," you may notice slight movements of their head in the other direction, such as shaking their head rather than nodding in agreement. It's signs like this that will give you the truth unconsciously every time, so make sure you're on the lookout for them.

Monitor Directional Behavior

Look out for the directional movements of the body someone has while speaking to you. When you're talking to someone you love about something honest and happy, the other person will unconsciously move forward and lean closer to you because they automatically want to be a deeper, more connected part of what's being said.

On the other hand, if someone is uncomfortable and uneasy about a situation, even if they had to sit in the situation and bear it, they will unconsciously move away. This could materialize in many ways, such as physically leaning away while sitting in a chair or facing a different direction. Imagine someone sitting with one leg folded over the other. Keep an eye on which way their knees are pointing.

If they are pointing at you, then they are listening and connecting with you. If they are pointing away from you, this can be a sign they're disconnected and want to get away. It's the same with the direction of their hands, the direction their feet are pointing, and so on.

Summary of Body Language

There are lots of ways you can use body language to read whether someone is lying to you, and it's important to remember that each sign on its own is not a guarantee that someone is lying, but more an indication that you should pay close attention to what they're saying because they could be lying to you.

Let's say you're having a conversation with your partner about a dent that has suddenly appeared on the side of the car. As you're talking and figuring out what happened, you notice a few of the signs. Your partner starts acting inconsistently with how they normally do. Their eyes are rapidly darting from side to side, and they're fidgeting by playing with something on the table.

Reading someone's body language is basically your first step in noticing that someone could be lying to you. It's in this moment when you've seen the signs that you should realize it's time to pay close attention to what is actually being said to you and trying to figure out a motive.

For now, just practice reading people and their body language and looking for the signs someone is lying to you. If you notice that someone is giving one or more of the signs, then try to figure out what motive someone could have to lie to you in what they're saying, as we discussed in the previous chapter.

You can then use the information in the next chapter to look for further signs depending on what's being said via verbal communication (aka, the actual content of the conversation).

Chapter Four - The Power of Words: Verbal Signs Someone is Lying to You

"There are people so addicted to exaggeration that they actually can't tell the truth without lying." - Josh Billings

The other person's body language is not the only giveaway you can keep your eyes open for. Sure, body language makes up around 55% of all communication (which is why we started with it!). Still, the actual verbal content remains a big part of it, averaging around 7%. Yeah, that might not seem like a lot, but it will vary depending on your source. Typically, the other 38% surrounds tone of voice, but we'll also dive into that throughout this chapter.

Basically, you need to be listening to what's being said to you in the context of the conversation you're having and how it's being said. There are obvious verbal signs that can prove someone's lying to you. Once you've noticed some of the body language signs and then some of these verbal signs, you'll be able to confirm that someone is being dishonest to you.

This chapter is all about diving into the tips and techniques that can help you highlight lies you're listening to and the nuances of accurate verbal communication. What's more, some of these techniques are highlighted and advised by people like Michael Floyd, an ex-CIA officer who has literally written the books on interrogation and getting the truth from people, such as his best selling book co-written by Philip Houston *Spy the Lie: Former CIA Officers Show You How to Detect When Someone is Lying*.

I mention a couple of his books throughout this book because these literally describe the techniques that the best, most professional, industry-leading lie-detecting humans are using, so let's take a look at them now!

Not Answering Statements

If you're speaking with someone and you find them failing to answer a question or statement you're presenting them, this could be a case where they're lying and trying to avoid further lying statements. When it comes to lying and getting away with it, the best lies are the ones that don't need a lot of detail and seem very natural. The more natural, the better. We'll explore this in more detail a little bit later on, but the basics are that the more detail you include in a lie, the more likely you are to be found out.

This makes sense. The more details and "truths" a lie has, the more detail someone has to work with and the more angles there are to be caught out on. This is why people who are lying can suddenly seem to stop mid-conversation and will be hesitant about giving more details, whether that's in the form of answering a question or continuing with their story. They don't want to add more dishonest details that could catch them out later.

If you notice that someone is failing to come up with a good answer or really doesn't want to carry on with the subject at hand, then this could be a clear indication that they're lying or at least trying to avoid telling you the truth.

Strange, Dramatized Denial

I've used the example of a child lying to their parents about something to avoid being told off or punished throughout this book, and that's because it's such a great example. Children have yet to understand the complexities of being human, so how they act and behavior is how we all act and behave, just in its purest, usually most unconscious, form.

This is prevalent in cases where you're asking them if they've done something wrong, and they'll deny it in such a way that proves that they're lying. This is because if someone, say, takes a chocolate biscuit before dinner and denies it, the denial is much more likely to be dramatized if it's a lie.

The conversation might go along the lines of:

"Did you take a chocolate biscuit out of the tin when I told you not to?"

"No."

This is what would happen if no lies were being told. On the other hand, the conversation would look a little more like this if they were lying:

"Did you take a chocolate biscuit out of the tin when I told you not to?"

"No! I didn't do it. I didn't take anything!"

This kind of dramatization can carry over into adult life, and I'm sure you're thinking of situations in your own life where you know someone is lying, and they dramatize their denial that they've done something wrong. While this isn't a guaranteed sign someone has lied, it's undoubtedly an indication that they could be.

Repeating the Question Again

A typical and commonly known sign someone is lying is when they repeat your question back to you, thus buying time for their response. Of course, they could simply be repeating the question back to ensure they heard it correctly. Still, it's usually an obvious situation where they've just misheard you.

However, if they're repeating the question and there's no way they would not have heard what you said the first time, keep your ears and eyes open for lies. People usually repeat a question or statement back to make it look like they haven't heard a question when really they're trying to think of a response that isn't the truth and need a little more time to think about it to make it plausible.

This is basically when the lie is being created, so make sure you always pay attention to what's being said after the repetition of your statement or question.

Saying Lots of Words but Not a Lot of Content

We all know someone who can go on and on about a subject for hours at a time, but when it comes down to a conversation, and someone is talking but not really saying too much, this can be an obvious sign that you're being lied to. This is because they're avoiding the direct and blunt truth of the matter.

Take these two sentences as an example in response to the question "Where did the money in your savings account go?"

"I was stupid and withdrew it all to go gambling."

"The money in my savings account? Which account are we talking about because I have two, and I think I actually have three because there's one connected with my current account, which I used to use all the time but haven't done recently. I do need to check up on that because I had a letter about it the other day...."

See how the latter answer has a lot of words, but there's not a lot of meaning? This kind of talk is known as "filler," and when someone is talking to you with a lot of filler statements but no real solid, firm points or context. Also, notice how there was a repetition of the question at the beginning? This all comes together to show that the person is lying, or at least trying to avoid telling the truth.

Some other key points to look out for include:

- Using phrases like "I'll be honest with you" and "To tell you the truth..."

- Using lots of filler words like "uh," "um," and "like"

Considering Tone of Voice

There's no doubt that the tone and quality of someone's voice is by far the most unreliable way to tell whether someone is lying. While it makes up a large percentage of all communication that we unconsciously look for, it can be difficult to judge someone's tone of voice and what it's saying without practice and without knowing the person you're speaking to.

However, there are clues you can use, such as:

- The pitch of someone's voice increasing

- Taking a long pause before they speak (considering what they're going to say next)

- Speaking slower, as if to give themselves more time to think through what they're saying

- A change in volume (typically, suddenly louder or quieter)

However, these aren't necessarily clear-cut signs someone is lying to you.

If you're talking to someone who's an effective communicator, these points could all be positive things. For example, someone may speak slowly to ensure they're being heard correctly. As with most of these points, have an awareness of someone's tone of voice as an indication that they could be lying. If you can match up multiple signs, then you know you may be on to something.

A Defensive Attitude

When you start talking about a subject that someone doesn't want to be involved with, you'll notice a huge shift in their attitude as they become very defensive. Let's say someone is cheating on their partner, but they have been using the excuse that they're not coming home on Friday nights because they've been asked to work late on a big project that's been going on for several months.

On the weekend, the partner who's being cheated on brings up the work conversation and asks how the project is going. Because they've been lying about the project and have really been seeing someone else, they become very defensive because they are resistant to talking about the topic, which can result in them saying things like:

"Work is hard enough as it is. I don't want to live it through again by talking about it with you. You really think I want to talk about it more?"

"Why do you want to know about work so much? It's just boring client work."

"Look, I don't want to talk about it because it's stressing me out so much as it is."

To start talking about a subject with someone who has lied about it is going to be taken as an attack on them, which is why they get defensive. The liar feels threatened. Other telltale signs of this could be them claiming you're wasting their time by talking about the situation, or they may switch the conversation around to you, trying to attack your character.

An example of this would be someone who's working on a project but has been procrastinating or went out over the weekend and finished no work. Instead, they told everyone they were ill, but they feel that their lie is being threatened when asked about it since people may find out the truth.

"So, have you done the work?"

"I told you, I'm going to get it done."

"We just really need it done. Are you feeling better?"

"Look, if you need it done so bad, why don't you do it? Have you got time to do it? You're healthy and not ill, right?"

Since they're attacking you and trying to make you feel bad, then chances are they're projecting how they feel about themselves on the inside. Especially in this example, the attacks are theatrical and unnecessary, signifying stress, a typical sign that someone is lying.

The More Detail, the More Chance They're Lying

We spoke about this point briefly above, but if someone is telling you a story and lying, they will tend to add a lot more details to the story to make it more convincing. Here's an example in which lying is likely not happening:

"Hey, why are you late to work?"

"Sorry, I was stuck in traffic."

Since you were stuck in traffic, this is really all that needed to be said. However, if you were lying and you were trying to be more convincing, the conversation could look a little more like this:

"Hey, why are you late to work?"

"I'm so sorry. You wouldn't believe what I had to go through to get here. The traffic was awful, and there was this red truck that kept cutting me off on the highway over and over again, and then there must have been a crash further down the road because all the lanes were backed up, and it's just a nightmare."

It's the excess of detail like the latter statement that clarifies that there's more to the story than just what's being said, ironically. In psychology, this is known as the "halo effect," which basically refers to someone's attempts to manage how they see you and what they believe.

To give you the lowdown on the halo effect, this psychological process was first documented back in 1920 in the article "Constant Error in Psychological Ratings," written by an American psychologist known as Edward Thorndike. Of course, the word halo has been used for its religious connotations (i.e., an angel or saint-like person who has a halo) or someone wanting to show how much of a positive person they are.

In short, someone will lie to you to make themselves seem like a better or at least a good person who does no wrong. The more they get away with that, the more lies of the same context they'll get away with over an extended period of time. This is when someone says, "John couldn't have done that! He's such a good person!" It's the manipulation of someone's own reputation.

In the context we're talking about, the halo effect is implemented to make someone seem like a reasonable person in the eyes of others. In the situation where someone is late to work, everything they explain in their lie is to make it seem like they tried their hardest and did everything in their power to get to work on time, but the world was seemingly against them. In other words, they claim that it's not their fault, and they are indeed the angel/saint-like person they want you to believe they are.

No matter what they say, they won't admit to doing anything wrong, nor will they own the fact that they made a mistake because it will harm their glorious reputation in the eyes of others. This is even if they did forget to set their alarm, slept through it, or just wanted to sit down and enjoy the rest of their breakfast while deciding what lie would be the most plausible to share as to why they arrived late.

This is an interesting concept because it states that the person is good in the eyes of others, but simply by association, you start to apply other positive characteristics and traits to that person, even if you have no knowledge or proof of them fulfilling the requirements to those traits.

This might sound a little confusing but bear with me. An example of this would be if someone lied about how hard they tried to get to work but couldn't because they were late. From this reasoning, you could believe that this person is a hardworking person in general, meaning they're also hardworking in the workplace. They go above and beyond the call of duty to get things done, supposedly.

Then when they lie about why they haven't handed in their report and give you every excuse under the sun, which we already know is going to highlight all the problems with the world and how they tried their hardest to meet the deadline but just couldn't do it, you're more likely to believe them. Thanks to the halo effect, the lies are consistent.

While it's interesting, the best thing for you to do is to actually listen to what people in your life and conversations are telling you. If you notice signs that they could be lying, then start looking for other lies that match the narrative they're sharing with you in the moment. You should begin to see similarities across the board.

Politeness in Overdrive

While perhaps not so common anymore, there are still many people out there who become slightly more polite when they're lying. This attempts to make the other person feel respected or to get the person being lied to, to like the liar more. The brain says, *If I can get this person to like me, then they won't think I'm lying to them because they'll be too caught up with how much they like me.*

This works exceptionally well if you know the person well and you notice this change in their personality, attitude, and the way they're talking to you, but it's definitely something you can look for when talking to strangers.

Use of Honest Language

This one may seem a little counterproductive, but when people overexaggerate that they're telling the truth, this could very well be a sign that they're lying to you. This is simply because the liar is trying to convince you that they're not lying. These statements can appear in many ways, but some of the most common statements you may hear include ones like:

> "I honestly believe the folder was over there."

> "I swear to God the wheel of my car was flat."

> "I'm not going to lie, the traffic on the way here was awful."

As with all the verbal and nonverbal signs of lying we've looked at over the last two chapters, it's essential to make sure you're not just using *one* of the signs as your way of determining whether someone is lying to you. One sign on its own is never usually enough and could appear for all manner of reasons. However, if you notice one, use that as an initial sign to look out for others.

Don't worry if you can't remember every single sign off the top of your head. Becoming decent at lie-spotting takes practice and awareness of knowing what to look out for and what signs people in your life have because everyone is different and will give away their lies in different ways.

Start noticing a stream of verbal signs mixed with body language giveaways. It could be time to think about how you're going to deal with the person who's lying to you—in other words, figuring out how you're being lied to and what the truth of the matter actually is. This is what we're looking at throughout the following chapters, which is where we're at right now!

Chapter Five - Probing for More: Ways to Find the Truth

"Truth is like the sun. You can shut it out for a time, but it ain't goin' away." - Elvis Presley

This is perhaps the most important part of this book. There are going to be numerous times in your life where you find yourself dealing with a liar. These could be little white lies, or they could be massive relationship-altering lies. It doesn't matter. In either situation, you're going to figure out, using the skills in the last two chapters, that the truth isn't being told.

For me personally, and I'll assume for you, there's a big difference between knowing whether someone is lying or not and actually figuring out the truth of what they're saying. You may call someone out on their lying ways yet find yourself still unable to get them to admit the facts of what's going on.

Of course, when you need to know the truth, there's nothing that should stop you from getting it, which is why I'm dedicating this whole chapter to finding out (and the next one as well, but more on that later!)

How to Start Digging for the Truth

In previous chapters, we've spoken about the importance of eye contact when it comes to detecting a lie and checking to see whether someone is comfortable while talking to you. They call eyes the "windows to the soul," and it's true. You could feel very disconnected from another human being you're speaking with, but the moment you make eye contact, everything changes. In the same vein, you can also use eye contact to get the truth.

In recent research carried out by the University of Tampere, there was an experiment conducted where participants played a computer game where they had to compete against other people in the study where they had to lie and tell the truth and figure out who was being honest or not, or to get away with being dishonest. As they played, the researchers monitored and tracked the participants' eye movements. As a result, the study found that making direct eye contact with other people was enough, in many cases, to stop them from lying while trying to win the game.

Using the results from this research, we can conclude that making eye contact with someone you're speaking to can be enough to stop them from lying to you in the first place or pressuring them when it comes to finding out the truth. This makes a lot of sense when you start picturing it in your day-to-day life.

Imagine you're talking to someone right now, and you're trying to get away with lying to them. What are you going to do with your eyes? Are you going to stare at them directly, or will you be looking at the floor? If you're like the vast majority of dishonest people, you're going to be looking everywhere other than their eyes because most humans find it so difficult to lie while making eye contact.

However, human beings find it naturally difficult to avoid making eye contact with others they're speaking to because of the connection we have with one another. This means that even when someone is lying, they'll be wanting to make eye contact with you unconsciously, but will be struggling to do so, which is what makes it so obvious. If you're able to maintain and apply pressure to a conversation by holding your eye contact with someone else, basically forcing them to keep eye contact, then there's going to be less of a chance you'll be lied to.

In the words of Robert Glatter, M.D., the assistant professor of emergency medicine at Lenox Hill Hospital:

"Making eye contact changes the dynamics of an interaction, turning it deeply personal, demanding accountability for their actions and behavior. Being direct in this fashion is a power move and asserts authority, respect, and accountability."

In other words, making eye contact with someone creates a personal connection that's hard to avoid. If you're not making eye contact with the person who's lying to you, then you're making it easy for them to get away with it.

However—and this is a big however—there are compulsive liars out there who will lie to your face, and they won't care if they're making eye contact with you. They're still going to lie their socks off and avoid telling you the truth. So, what can you do about it? Let's find out, and we'll start with the basics.

Avoid Being in a Crowd

Remember, if someone's lied to you, you don't need to get them to tell the truth in the same interaction. You can take your time to find out over a longer period of time, which is essential for this point. Nobody wants to be singled out for their lying tendencies in front of a crowd of people because this will be far more embarrassing and humiliating. If mentioned, the chances are they'll only solidify themselves in the lie further while becoming very defensive. In other words, you're not going to make any progress.

Instead, if you suspect someone's lying, it's always going to be best to talk to them about it in a private, one-on-one environment. It's good to remember that not all lies are malicious, and some people may be trying to protect themselves or other people, even though the lies could be causing more harm than the liar actually realizes.

Meet in a one-on-one meeting and make the other person feel comfortable. Michael Floyd, the CIA operator and author of *Former CIA Officers Teach You How to Persuade Anyone to Tell All,* also recommends bringing food to your meeting or at least eating out somewhere. This is because many people will associate food with pleasure, making you come across as more likable. This means the liar is more likely to open up and be honest with you.

Avoid Aggression at All Costs

Put yourself in the position of a liar. Again, not all lies are malicious or incredibly horrible, not in the grand scheme of things. You could lie because you're embarrassed that you broke something or missed an appointment for a silly reason you don't want to admit to anyone. Remember the motives we spoke about before? If you're caught for your lying, and you're called on it, how are you going to react if someone comes at you aggressively?

You're going to shut down, get defensive, and you won't want to open up, and this is precisely how other people are going to react. If the lie you've been told is hurtful, then sure, it might not be easy to remain cool, calm, and collected yourself, but you must invoke your emotional intelligence and stay as grounded as you can.

If you can approach people in such a way that will keep them comfortable and feeling safe (in other words, not attacked), then you're far more likely to get the actual truth out of them.

Get the Person Back to the Present Moment

It's understandable that when someone lies and feels as though they're getting caught, they're going to "clam up" and feel uncomfortable. Remember the times you've lied and been caught lying, even if it was over something small? And as soon as you started feeling as though you'd been caught or would get harassed for your lie, what did you do? You withdrew into yourself.

It's quite a common stereotype that people will actually break down and start crying, dramatizing their emotions so other people will feel empathy and compassion for them when really they're just incredibly scared that people will find out the truth. They start crying to draw people away from the chance of this happening. You've probably seen this happen in the movies.

As a rule of thumb, when liars start thinking about the long-term consequences of their lie, they're going to seize up and withdraw into themselves because they don't want to be caught, making it much harder to find out the truth.

Instead, focus on sharing statements that promote short-term thinking. You could say things like:

"Don't worry, everyone makes mistakes from time to time. It's how we deal with them that makes us good people."

"Good people do stupid things. We're only human."

"All problems are fixable once we know what we're dealing with. Let's sort it out."

And so on. These statements will help the liars not feel the need to retreat but instead encourage them to face the truth and thus share it with you.

Act Like You Know the Truth

By acting like you know the truth, I don't mean pretending to know exactly what's going on. I mean, don't harass the person you're speaking to with questions that creates the impression you're trying to dig deeper and deeper into their dishonesty.

This comes back to making the liar feel as though they're being attacked. Again, even if the lies they've told have been incredibly hurtful to you, it's important you invoke your emotional intelligence and stay in control in order to get to the truth.

Instead of harassing the other person with questions, create an ongoing monologue. This makes the liar think that you know exactly what's going on. You're not so much caught up on the details that they've lied to you, but that you are aware of the situations and the pressures relating to it, but are more focused on getting things fixed and sorted out, but this needs to begin with them telling you the truth.

Here's an example of this in action.

Person One: We just need to find out who took the money. The quicker we can get it back, the quicker this whole situation will be over.

Person Two: I told you, I don't know who took it or where it went. I don't know how many times I have to tell you.

As this conversation is happening, Person One sees that Person Two's body language suggests they're lying.

Person One: If we're able to find out who did it, that doesn't mean the person is going to get in trouble. All we basically want is for the money to be returned. Whoever took the money obviously had their reasons for doing it. Maybe we'll also be able to help them out as well. We want nothing more in this situation than to sort the problems out.

Person Two: Yeah. I know what you mean.

Person One: Look, I don't want to accuse you of doing something you didn't do, but I also really don't want you to feel like you have to lie if you did and bottle up all the negative feelings that come with lying. If you did take the money, I'm not here to punish you or make you look bad. I just want to morally sort things out.

Person Two: Yes. Okay. I took the money. I'm sorry. I just saw it, and I don't know what came over me.

And so on. This is an important lesson I'm sure we can all learn from. What with the rise in movements like "Cancel Culture" and penalizing people for the things they've done wrong, so many of us want to play "gotcha!" and catch people who have done wrong or who have been dishonest and punish them for being bad people. Take a look at the other approach you could use.

Person One: We just need to find out who took the money. The quicker we can get it back, the quicker this whole situation will be over.

Person Two: I told you, I don't know who took it or where it went. I don't know how many times I have to tell you.

Person One: Look, just own up to it. Who took it? Did you take it? Do you know who took it?

Person Two: Why are you harassing me so much? How do we know you didn't take it and you're trying to pin it on someone else? Maybe you lost it because you're so careless.

Not a productive approach, and now the conversation has escalated into a conflict.

Again, not all people who lie are bad, and they will have their reasons. Isn't it a much more beneficial approach to try and sort out problems and overcome them productively than trying to bring people down and make them suffer? I, for one, believe there's already too much of that in the world, and a more compassionate approach is always going to bring about better, more productive results.

Now, this can feel like pandering. If your partner cheats on you and lies about it, you finding out the truth is going to hurt a lot, and it's going to make you reactive. Granted, but I'll talk about this a little later on at the end of this chapter.

Don't Accuse People

This point goes hand in hand with not being aggressive towards people and comes in the form of accusing people of the things they've supposedly done or lied about. Check out this table for some ideas for things you can say that can feel accusing and other ways to say the same thing, but in a way that's presumptive and constructive.

The Accusing Statement	The Presumptive Statement
Why did you take the money?	Do you know where the money is?
Why have you cheated on me?	Is there something I need to know about our relationship?

Did you take the jewelry from my drawer?	Is there anything taken from my room I need to know about?
Why did you lie to me?	Is there anything you've been dishonest about that I should know?
Why are you late to work?	How was your morning getting into work?
Did you call Mary a pig behind her back?	Did you maybe say something to Mary out of anger?

Accusing people in an attacking manner will only shut them down and make them want to withdraw into themselves. You may not feel like being civil if you're being lied to, but a productive and beneficial conversation won't occur unless you can be this way. If you do feel aggressive, take a step back and allow your emotions to calm down before approaching the dishonest person.

Utilize Your Own Body Language

While you're going to be reading someone else's body language to see whether they're lying to you throughout your conversations, you can also use your body language to communicate how you're feeling, but is it possible to do this in such a way when you're trying to find out the truth? Of course you can, and there's a relatively simple method you can learn.

By simply raising your hand at certain points in your conversations, you're telling the other person they need to stop talking and think about what they're saying. This is commonplace since raising your hand, like someone who's directing traffic would do, is a universal sign for stop.

Let's say someone is lying to you, and you've read the signs and know this to be the case. If you ask a presumptive question, as I spoke about in the previous section, and the person continues to lie, you can simply raise your hand to give the signal that you want them to stop talking. Naturally, they will pick up on these signals and stop while receiving the message that you know they're lying and don't want to hear what they have to say because you know it's not the truth.

Using methods like this, you're not actually accusing the other person of lying aggressively. You're not calling them out or shaming them but instead giving a subtle indication that you know what's up and aren't interested in carrying on in this way. Rather, you want to get to the truth and get the situation sorted.

A Note on Communicating with Liars

As I was writing this chapter, I kept thinking about what it takes to actually talk to a liar. Using the example I gave earlier in the chapter, let's say your partner has cheated on you but is lying about it, or someone at work is lying to you about working on a project, and it's left you feeling incredibly frustrated. Maybe even a friend lied to you about taking money from you while they visited your home.

All of these situations will feel infuriating, but a lot of what we've spoken about means you have to stay cool, calm, and collected while ensuring you're being patient with the other person. This is hard. It can feel as though you're catering and pandering how you communicate to suit the person you're talking to. The thought of giving them empathy and compassion might make you feel as though they haven't done the same to you, especially if they're lying to you. You may feel bitter and think, *Why do I have to be nice to this person when they've been horrible, immoral, and dishonest to me?*

While you may want to "flip out," rage, and accuse someone of lying, venting how aggressive you feel to the person who's hurt you, the truth of the matter is that this is never going to be a solution that leads to a positive result. Sure, you may get your "revenge," but you're never going to make things better. In fact, you're almost always going to make things worse.

If you're acting out of emotion and being a mindless kind of person, everyone involved is going to be aggressive, defensive, or untruthful. You can't fight fire with fire.

You are an emotionally intelligent human being. If you haven't mastered being emotionally intelligent yet, it's certainly something you can work towards. Being emotionally intelligent means you can stay focused and grounded the large majority of the time, even in the most intense conversations, such as one about you finding out your partner cheated on you.

Sure, being in such a situation can make you livid, but have the conversation calmly. Then you can take action on how you proceed, whether you're forgiving the other person or ending the relationship. The choice of how you respond to a lie is up to you, and if you want to shout and scream and vent, you can choose to do so, but the point is that you made the choice to act that way, and you're not just mindlessly interacting with people.

If you want the best results out of the conversation where you're finding out what's fact and what's fiction, then you need to approach the situation in the most grounded way possible. Here are a few quick-fire tips on how to bring more emotional intelligence into your everyday life:

- Practice tuning in and becoming aware of your emotions and how you feel throughout the day. Check in yourself and write down how you feel. With practice, you'll be able to do this in more intense situations where you can say to yourself, "Hold on, I'm feeling angry; how is this going to affect how I act?"

- Take responsibility. How you feel and how you act in the world and towards others is entirely within your control. Take responsibility for your actions and realize how much power you have in the decisions you make every day, even in the most minute ways.

- Don't ignore negative feelings. It's perfectly valid to feel negative emotions, like hate, anger, and sadness. Being emotionally intelligent is not about being positive and calm all the time, but recognizing when the negative emotions come up and then being able to accept them for what they are.

- Realize your motives. No matter what you're saying or doing, try to identify your motive for doing it. If you want to shout and scream at someone, ask yourself why this is the action you want to take. Is it an action you actually want to do, or are you going to regret it? Is there a better action you can take that will be more beneficial to you and everyone around you? Being emotionally intelligent is about being able to put yourself in a position where you're capable of asking these kinds of questions.

- You will make mistakes. Even the most emotionally intelligent people in the world will slip up and act mindlessly from time to time. We are all only human, after all. The best people understand that being emotionally intelligent is not something you get to and then stay there forever, but that it's a lifelong process where you're continually growing and learning.

There's a lot you can go into when it comes to being emotionally intelligent, so much so I could write a whole book on that alone, but these should be enough to get you started. In short, stop acting mindlessly in your life and start taking control of the things you can control, like the things you say and the actions you do. It's a lack of these skills in other people that had them lying in the first place, so don't stoop to their level. Be better!

Summary of Finding Out the Truth

We've covered a lot in this chapter, and at this point, you should have all the skills and knowledge you need to know when it comes to finding out the truth when talking to anyone, not just a liar. These are skills that can be applied to anyone at any time. Remember, some people won't even be directly lying to you but will instead be avoiding the truth. However, these are still techniques you can implement into these interactions to get to the bottom of what's going on.

Some of them may come naturally to you, and some of these techniques you may need a little practice, but the real trick is just to be mindful of what these techniques are and try them out here and there. With experience, you'll get better and better at using them and finding out the truth.

Now, I know what you're thinking. That's a lot of techniques to remember and think about, and is it even possible to have a natural conversation when you're trying to think about everything we've spoken about in the last couple of chapters? It is, but while being mindful of everything we've spoken about, our next chapter is all about narrowing it down into an easy five-step guide to help you find out the truth in any situation.

Chapter Six - An Easy Five-Step Guide to Finding the Truth

"Love is nothing other than finding the truth." - *Rumi*

Understandably, there's a lot of nuances to think about when it comes to finding out the truth, and since everyone is different, people will have different signs that they're lying. It can be a lot to think about, but fortunately, there's a technique you can use to figure out whether anybody is lying to you using the basic signs. In fact, this is a method known as the BASIC method, as described in Pamela Meyer's best-selling book, *Liespotting*.

Pamela is an author and fraud investigator with a TED talk on spotting liars and finding out the truth that has been watched over 25 million times and sits as one of the top-20 all-time favorite TED talks ever recorded. She has studied the psychology of lying in Harvard and other universities for decades, compiling her knowledge into her book, which has sold thousands of copies.

In other words, Pamela knows what she's talking about, so if you're interested, make sure to read her book for yourself. However, I'm going to give you an edited version of her BASIC lie-detecting method you can apply in any conversation with anyone (especially since Pamela's method is designed around spotting lies in high-stakes business deals), so let's get right into it.

Step One - Consider Standard Behaviors

There is a psychological technique known as baselining, which is something we've generally spoken about already. Baselining is the process of getting to know the people in your life and understanding how they averagely act on a day-to-day basis. For example, if your colleague is a bit quiet and doesn't really talk, if he only nods at you when you say hello, then you define that as being his baseline. He's the quiet, humble type.

If your partner gets stressed out when there are lots of things to do on the to-do list, such as when you're getting ready to go on vacation, then you know this is your partner's baseline behavior, and there's nothing out of the ordinary when they act this way.

For example, with my father, I knew he was practically useless in the mornings for doing anything until he had his morning coffee at ten o'clock, after which he would be functional for the rest of the day. If I came downstairs in the morning at nine and he was grumpy, this was nothing out of the ordinary because of what his baseline said about him.

Using the skills you've already learned when it comes to monitoring body language and verbal communications, you know when someone isn't meeting their baseline behaviors and when they're acting out of the ordinary. When this happens, you can start to figure out that they might be lying to you, or at least something is going on.

This could come in the form of someone doing some of the behaviors you know they do when they lie (verbal or nonverbal).

For example, there used to be a guy who worked in the same office as me who would start to stutter whenever he told a lie. He would stagger his sentences until he had to take a deep breath, reset, and then try again. It's almost as though the process of lying overwhelmed him. Whenever lunches were missing from the fridge, and he started to stutter while saying it wasn't him, then we knew it most certainly was.

Of course, the baseline behavior for everybody in your life will be different. Some people may laugh when they're nervous or will go quieter than usual. Some people will pick at their fingernails or cuticles. Your goal in Step One is to become aware of when the people in your life are deviating from their baseline.

Some key traits to keep your eyes open for include things like:

- A change in the person's laugh, whether that's tone, volume, or style

- A change in the person's posture, regardless of whether they're sitting or standing

- Any changes to their voice, including the tone, pitch, and speed

- Are they making any gestures they wouldn't usually make?

- Does the person have the right reactions to the conversation that's happening?

Another example of this would be if you're talking about something sensitive, like someone losing their job or a pet passing away. Suppose the person isn't as emotional or distressed about the situation as they would normally be. If their reactions don't meet the baseline you have for them, then the chances are something is up.

Step Two - Asking Open Questions

By following Step One, you should have a very clear idea when someone is lying to you. Your gut instinct and all your training so far are making you believe that something is up, so where do you go from here? It's time to start questioning what's going on and to start getting some answers.

Using what we spoke about in the last chapter, it's not a good idea to start by asking aggressive, accusing questions that will put the other person on the spot and make them withdraw into themselves. Instead, you need to focus on asking open-ended questions that allow the other person to own up to what they're doing. You're hinting to the other person that you know they're lying and allowing them to come forward with the truth.

By an open-ended question, I mean one that can't just be answered with a simple yes or no response since these create the opportunity for the lie to be bypassed. Some examples of closed-ended questions you'll want to avoid include things like:

> "Did you take the money?"
>
> "Did you meet the deadline?"
>
> "Did you pay the bill?"
>
> "Did you cheat on your boyfriend?"
>
> "Did you steal the phone?"

Instead, you can transform these questions into open-ended questions that allow for a much clearer response.

By transforming the questions above, these statements become:

"Do you know where the money could be?"

"How did you manage to meet the deadline?"

"How did you pay for the bill?"

"Do you see why people would think you're cheating on your boyfriend?"

"Where is the phone?"

By asking questions like this, you're creating the opportunity for the other person to be honest. Of course, this doesn't mean they will be, but you're creating a gap in thinking where the other person can think, *Okay, I'm lying, but now is my chance to come clean and get it all out in the open.* If you ask a close-ended question, like "Did you steal the phone?" they can just say no without any extra thought.

As described by Pamela, there are four main goals you're going to want to think about when asking open-ended questions.

Goal One - Clarify Your Goal

Firstly, you need to decide what it is you want to find out. If you're addressing the issue of a missing phone, your overall aim is to find the location of the phone, so there's no point in asking questions like "Why would you take the phone?" or "Why do you think someone would want to take the phone?" These feel somewhat like productive questions, but they only achieve in bringing the conversation off course.

Instead, focus on questions that are going to get you the cold hard facts that will lead to the subject's conclusion. Make sure you're not assuming anything right away, even if you're full of suspicion, and use the five standard question types (who, what, why, when, and how) to lead the conversation in the direction you want it to go.

When asking the questions, make sure you're using accepting body language that shows you're clearly inquiring into the topic, not accusing the other person, thus making them defensive. You could so easily do this by crossing your arms or placing your hands on your hips in an aggressive way, so keep your arms open and make kind eye contact.

For clarity, some tips to remember here are:

- Mirror the other person's body language to make them feel connected and open to you

- Keep an appropriate amount of eye contact when asking your questions

- Use non-threatening and non-aggressive body language

- Avoid argumentative conversation tones at all costs

Goal Two - Connect with the Other Person

Through active listening and using the body language tips we spoke about a second ago, you can start to connect with the person you're talking to. This is good because the greater your connection to the other person, the more likely they'll be to open up to you.

Again, if you're coming across in a hostile and aggressive fashion, then the other person is going to get defensive and will shut down. However, if you can come across in a friendly way, they'll be much more likely to open up to you and tell you the truth. I know I keep talking about this, but that's because it's so important! I can say it a million times now, but you can bet the first time you find yourself in a situation where you're being lied to, it's going to be so difficult to remember. Keep drumming it in!

Anyway, this entire process can also be described as developing rapport, which is one of the most important goals in this process.

Decide what kind of language you're using in your conversation. If you come straight out and say something like, "Someone has stolen my phone. Who was it?" even using the word stolen can freak the person out and will contribute to them panicking and shutting down. Instead, saying something like "It seems my phone is missing" is a much more approachable way to word the statement.

Again, this can feel like you're pandering to the liar, but this way, you can get the truth first, then decide what you're going to do once you know the facts.

Instead of attacking the other person, you need to connect and open them up. Remember, every liar has a motive behind what they're doing and a story they're telling themselves to justify why they're lying in the first place. In some cases, they could be trying to protect somebody else. While they may even want to tell the truth, they may have made a promise they don't want to break, perhaps even out of fear of being hurt themselves. These situations can be more complicated than you first believe, which is why you don't assume anything first.

Empathize with the liar by identifying possible motives to a lie and understanding the story they could tell you. For example, someone who stole money from work could be a really malicious person who's just a criminal with a criminal's mindset. On the other hand, they could be stealing money because they're really struggling and need money to feed their children and can't think of any other rational ways to deal with their stressful situation. You would need to approach both of these situations differently.

To summarize, put yourself in the shoes of the other person, and while you don't want to assume automatically that the other person is lying, connect with them to see why they could be lying and what they could be getting out of it. Once you're able to empathize in this way, you'll become far more approachable, and the other person becomes far more likely to tell you the truth.

This is a step in the right direction.

Step Three - Compile All the Signs

We've spoken about this point a lot, so I'll be quick for clarity.

It's important to remember that the individual signs on their own don't really mean a lot. If someone is fidgeting, playing with their hair, looking in another direction, or seems a bit tense or uncomfortable, this could literally mean anything. They might be having a bad day, might be nervous about an upcoming meeting or situation, or have something catch their eye while speaking with you.

However, step three is all about noticing all the signs and bringing them together. As you speak through the first two steps, you may notice they're not making a lot of eye contact, or they're playing with their nails or cuticles. While seemingly meaningless, should you notice these signs, you now need to keep your eyes open for others.

This is a process sometimes referred to as "studying the clusters" because you're literally looking for clusters of signs, and this includes both verbal and nonverbal signs that we spoke about in the last chapter.

Step Four - Look for the Gaps

Perhaps the most interesting step of Pamela's BASIC technique is this one. It involves looking for gaps in the other person's logic, thus identifying when they are lying. At this point in the conversation, you're fairly certain you're being lied to because all the signs are there, and you've consciously named them all. This is the part of the process where you're figuring out how you're being lied to. When you can figure this out, you know what lie is being told, ultimately taking you one step towards finding out the truth.

So, let's take a look at the gaps you need to look for in your conversations.

Statement Gap	This gap refers to the difference in continuity that occurs between what someone says they were doing and what they were actually doing.
	For example, if someone comes into the room in a hurry, and you ask what they were painting, and they say they weren't painting, but they have a paintbrush in their hand, this is a clear statement gap.
Logic Gap	A logic gap refers to strange events that come to light that can suggest that something doesn't quite add up.
	For example, if you've asked your partner to pay a bill, a bill they've always paid, and they say, "I am waiting for the

	confirmation code to come via email," but you know there's never been the need for a confirmation code before, this creates a logic gap.
Behavior Gap	The behavior gap process goes back to what we were talking about in step one and baselining the behaviors and actions of other people.
	For example, if someone says they get so incredibly exhausted when they're out socializing for too long with other people, but you see them being the life and soul of the party for hours at a time, this is a behavior gap.
Emotional Gap	If something doesn't add up emotionally when talking to the other person, then you know something is up. For example, they could be acting like your best friend and saying all the

right things, but if you catch them in a big sigh and look uncomfortable when your back is turned, this could be the sign of an emotional gap.

Emotional gaps are typically the hardest to spot because this is the gap type that people will be most conscious about hiding, but if you can spot them, then you'll be much closer to finding out the truth of a situation.

These four gap types are basically your keys to figuring out whether someone is lying to you and can be applied in pretty much any situation. Let's say you doubt the loyalty of your partner and you're trying to figure out whether they're cheating on you with someone else (I know I use this example a lot. I'm not trying to make you doubt your relationship, but it's just a great example where someone can hide their ways using all manner of lies and deceit).

For example, if your partner is always on their phone and you see them texting from the other sofa, you may simply ask, "Who are you texting?" If they reply with "Oh, no one," then this is a behavior gap because you know that they were texting. You literally just saw it with your own eyes, and this is where borderline gaslighting comes into play.

You may ask, "Hey, what are you up to?" to which they respond, "I'm just playing a game," you might think nothing of it, but then if you know your partner is not the sort of person to play games because they aren't interested in them, then this is a logic gap because why would they be playing games when they don't normally?

If your partner comes home late one night and you ask where they've been, and they simply reply, "I've just been working late," does the statement add up? If you know the company doesn't allow people to work in the office on their own due to health and safety reasons, then this is a statement gap because who else was working there with them? Why would they work late off their own back when previous experience tells you that your partner doesn't really like their job?

I know what you're thinking: *Damn, it's so easy to sound paranoid,* and when you put it all together like this, yes, it may seem that way. However, I want to remind you that not everyone will be lying to you all the time. These are the techniques you're going to want to use when you're suspecting that someone is lying to you or you're aware of the signs, so you know exactly what to look out for to detect lies as they're being told.

Again, your partner playing on their phone or texting someone else doesn't mean they're cheating on you. Yes, perhaps they're playing a Facebook game for the first time because they've found one they enjoy. There's no reason to be suspicious of that. But, if you're also seeing the verbal and nonverbal signs that you're being lied to, then this is where you'll need to start addressing your suspicions.

Step Five - Make Your Judgement

The final, most important step: Confirming that you're being lied to and then doing something about it.

Firstly, I need to stress that this doesn't mean you need to jump out of your chair, thrust your finger into the other person's face, and scream "I caught you!" at the top of your voice. Remember, you're an emotionally intelligent person that can deal with things in a grounded, collected way.

Paradoxically, the truth is that you may never actually find out the truth of what you're being lied to about. When I was 18, I had a girlfriend who moved away for college. We suffered the strains of a long-distance relationship, and as the weeks went by, we started to grow apart. It was a hard time, and we tried making the relationship work, but I had this nudging suspicion that she was too nervous about breaking up with me and couldn't bring herself to do it, but was still sleeping with other people in true college fashion.

She denied it over and over again, although it never satisfied my doubts. Eventually, I went to visit her for the weekend. While she was in the shower getting ready for a night out in the city, I saw a text ping through on her phone from the same guy I had my doubts about. The text was somewhat graphic and confirmed everything.

Now, in this situation, I never did find out whether my ex *physically* cheated on me or was just flirting over text messages or whatever. In this situation, I didn't really want to know the truth, but I was grateful (in hindsight) for finding out that I was being lied to. In some situations, you'll want the whole truth and nothing but the truth, and in others, just finding out you're being lied to will be enough for you to make your decision of what to do next. It all depends on the context of the situation and how you're feeling at the time.

And that's really the whole purpose of this book. It's to help you develop the skills you need to know to help you gather the truthful data of what people are communicating to you in this life, enabling you to make well-rounded, balanced, and founded decisions to help you have the present and future you want. That's the dream, right?

When making your final judgment and determining whether someone is lying to you, there are a few things you can do and be aware of to help make the process easier.

Seek the Truth

A quick reminder of what I spoke about in Step Two. Remember, the whole BASIC process is about finding out the truth, or lack of, so everything from the questions you're asking to the statements you make should be said with this goal in mind.

If you're unsure of whether someone is telling you the truth, make sure you're repeating the same question that helps you discover the facts of a situation. Just keep rewording it in a different way until you receive a straight answer.

If you suspect someone stole money from another friend while at a garden party over the weekend, and you're trying to figure whether someone did, you could ask multiple questions with the same goal. For example:

"So, what did you get up to on Sunday?"

"How did you find the party?"

"What did you do at the party? I didn't see you much."

"What time did you leave?"

Question any recent purchases that have been made.

And so on. You've probably seen this technique used in crime shows where the interrogator or detective will interview the criminal and will use various questions along the same lines trying to probe the person into sharing the truth. This is the same logic here.

Bring Emotion into the Picture

By questioning how the other person feels about the situation you're talking about, not only are you giving yourself the opportunity to look for emotional gaps, you're bringing yourself one step closer to finding out the truth. You can do this by literally asking the person how they feel.

"How do you feel about Andy's money stolen at his own party?"

"How would you feel if you threw a party and had your money stolen?"

"How do you feel about one of our friends being a thief?"

Not only are you giving the person a chance to respond emotionally by focusing on the subject, but the guilt alone could lead them into admitting what they've done or at least bring them one step closer to being in this position, but you're looking for those gaps.

When asked the latter question, any innocent, respectable friend would say something along the lines of:

"I know, right? It's awful. I can't believe someone would do that. They must be so desperate, and it's a real shame they don't feel like they're able to come to us for help, but instead have to try and steal behind our backs."

But a guilty person will be defensive and try to avoid the emotional aspect of this question, perhaps saying something like:

"Yeah. It's pretty bad."

This emotional gap and dismissive response are not what you would expect from someone who cares about their friend, which is why this can be such a powerful and revealing technique to use.

Focus on Consequences

Bringing to light the consequences of a bad action is another fantastic way to highlight guilty people. When asking someone what a consequence of a bad action could be, an innocent person will, of course, share ideas of an ideal punishment. On the other hand, a guilty person will obviously be far more lenient about the action (because they did it themselves and don't want to get in trouble) or will dismiss the question entirely.

"Well, someone took the money. It will be interesting to see what happens when the person is caught."

Innocent person: "Well, I for one know that I'll think long and hard about whether I even want to stay friends with them. How could we stay friends when we can't even trust them around our own personal belongings?"

Guilty person: "Yeah. It will."

Focus on Motives

When conversing with an innocent person about a situation where you're trying to find out the truth, they'll surely be happy to engage in a conversation where you try and figure out the motives of the person who has done something wrong. Are they greedy? Do they hate the person they stole from? Are they desperate for money? Do they need it because they're struggling for food or because they wanted the new iPhone?

On the other hand, a guilty person will be far less likely to engage in the conversation, may dismiss it altogether (because it's too close for comfort and may give the real reason away), or they'll offer up a story that is weak, unfounded, or highlights a gap that we spoke about before.

Dive Back into the Story

It's common knowledge that when someone lies, they will tell a story in chronological order (the order in which the events happened) because they're basically making it up as they go along. Even fabricated stories created in preparation for the conversation will be created in chronological order to confirm that the story makes sense and everything adds up.

However, this can cause problems when trying to recall certain aspects of the story and is one of the main areas of concern where liars can be caught. In the missing money example, you may ask your friend about what they did at the party, to which they'll respond with someone like:

Arrived > Got drinks > Danced > Sat outside > Danced some more > Went home.

When you jump back into a random part of the story and ask who they were outside with, because you're breaking the story up, you're making it far more likely that inconsistencies are going to appear. Especially in this example, you're asking them to call out people they were with, which is dangerous for a liar because there's no reason why you can't go and ask the other person to see if that was true.

However, the real results from this part of the technique come from reversing the order of the story. In this case, you're asking who they were outside with and what they were doing, and then you're asking, "Hold up, what did you do before going outside?"

Since most liars will have fabricated their story in chronological order, it's far harder for them to remain consistent when reversing the events or to jump back in at a random point.

If you notice hesitation here, thinking time, or signs of awkwardness (the typical lying signs we've already discussed), this could tell you everything you need to know. Any innocent person will be able to tell you fairly quickly what they were up to because they're simply recalling the truth.

Make Your Final Decision

As I said in the introduction of this step, you may never find out the actual truth of a situation, but you're surely going to find out that you're being deceived. If the person doesn't own up to what they've said or done, but you're convinced it happened, and all the facts point towards the result that you're being lied to, well, the ball's now in your court.

It's up to you what you do next. You could directly call the person out, telling them that you think they're lying, and see how they respond. Or, you could take a different approach. Maybe you need to converse with the people around you to see what decision you want to take. Or perhaps the whole situation was too stressful, and since it was caused by the words or actions of the other person, you've decided you just don't want that kind of person in your life.

Perhaps due to the perceived motives of the other person, you can forgive them and move on, developing your relationship to be stronger than ever before. Whatever happens, you know you're making your final decision based on facts and evidence where you know you've taken the time to get as close to the truth as possible.

Summary of the BASIC Technique

Bringing everything together that we've covered in the last four chapters, you now know the *complete* process when it comes to spotting liars in your everyday life. Phew! I know. There's a lot there, and your mind is probably reeling from all the information you've just onboarded. Don't worry, like every other aspect of life, spotting the liars in your life is something you'll get better at with practice, which means you need to try and implement it where you can and develop your skills over time. Because that's what lie-spotting is. It's a skill that needs to be learned and mastered over time, not just gut instinct or chance.

Unfortunately, it's not something you can just hone overnight. Just try to take your training one skill at a time. Learn about the BASIC process. Practice asking deeper, more focused questions to the people in your life, even when you think they're telling the truth, just to get an idea of how it works and to be confident in doing so.

With regular practice, you'll start to see an improvement in your communication skills and your awareness of other people, what they're saying, and their verbal and nonverbal communications, as well as their behavioral baselines. It all comes together with practice.

Chapter Seven - Mastering the Art of Lie-Spotting in Day-to-Day Life

"Finding out the truth is only half of it. It's what you do with it that matters." - Tristan Wilds

You know the process of how to spot a lie when it comes up in your life, and you also know how to find out the truth. You know how to get from being told a lie to then decide what to do about it. However, as with all things in life, this can be easier said than done. While you know the skills and techniques needed to figure out a lie, this chapter is all about *mastering* that skill.

This is no doubt a beefy chapter. There is a lot that's going to happen here as I dive into tips you need that will improve your lie-spotting skills in all areas and will help you dive deeper into the truth. Remember, you don't need to memorize everything we're going to talk about here and now, but rather take on a little at a time and apply your teachings when necessary.

Steer Clear of Denial Lockdowns

When you're conversing with someone who's really flat out denying that they didn't do something nor told a lie (even if you're convinced that they did), you can quickly end up in a situation that we call "denial lockdown." At first, you may have called someone out on their lying and, without even thinking, they just came out and said, "I didn't do it."

However, since they've already said they didn't do it (even though this was a lie), they have now committed to the lie of denial, and no matter what happens, no matter how ridiculous and heated the conversation gets, they have to stick to their guns and continue to deny it, regardless of how silly this could make them seem. They've said their part, and now they need to defend it.

Denial lockdown is very common in a situation where you get aggressive with your statements, and the other person gets defensive, and it's a very difficult situation to get out of. This is why I've been talking about avoiding it for so long! Instead, you need to make sure you're avoiding this kind of conversation altogether, or you need to use your communicative skills to guide the conversation back to a productive standpoint.

Basically, you need to do this however you can, even if you have to interrupt the person talking. If someone is insistently saying "I didn't do it!" over and over again, then you can interrupt and say, "Okay, I hear you," and then calmly go into why you think they did and your case, and then give them the time of day to hear their side in a calm and collected way.

You're never going to get anywhere with a tense, heated, and argumentative conversation.

Always Listen to the Other Person

When you've consciously decided that someone is lying to you, it can be hard to focus on anything but these feelings, which means that even when that person is trying to defend themselves, you're not actually listening to what they have to say because why should you? It's all lies anyway, right?

Well, not entirely. As an intelligent human being, it's important that even though you have your own judgments and perceptions, you're still able to put these thoughts and feelings to the side to actually hear what the other person is going to say. It's incredibly narrow-minded to do otherwise.

Yes, it can be hard to listen to other people properly, but if you're not willing to listen and have a proper conversation, then there's no point in having the conversation at all, and you may as well not bother and just come up with your ideas about people and live your life that way without even giving people a chance. You don't need me to tell you that you're in for a very unhappy life if you choose to live this way.

As a top tip, always try to clear your mind and listen to the other person speak. Hear their stories and their point of view and try to keep your mind free from judgment until they've finished and you've heard it all. If you're not clear about something, then make sure you're asking questions for clarity. Here are some tips on how to excel in this consideration:

- Be an active listener, not someone who listens to respond. In other words, listen to everything the other person has to say and then formulate your response. Don't just hold on to what you're trying to say to force your point.

- If you feel emotion or judgment taking over you, become mindful of these feelings and don't allow them to cloud your judgment or harm your ability to listen.

- Ask questions if you want to clarify a point someone has made or you don't understand something. This shows you're listening and makes the other person feel respected, making them far more likely to open up and talk to you honestly.

- Listen more effectively with open body language. This means making an appropriate amount of eye contact, turning your body to look in the direction of the person you're speaking, and adopting open and non-aggressive body language. This means not sitting with your legs crossed, not crossing your arms, and keeping a relaxed expression.

Practice on Honest People

Just another quick tip to consider here. While you may want to practice all these tips on people who are lying to you, there's no reason why you can't practice on people who are simply telling you the truth. Try reading the body language of people who are just generally talking to you and try to figure out what they're trying to say and how they're feeling.

When someone is speaking comfortably and honestly, you notice the opposite of all the signs I've spoken about already, and this is a very good technique for helping you benchmark what certain people are like and how they act naturally in conversations.

Body Language Tends to Be Clearer than Verbal Signs

When someone is heading into a situation they know to be tense, then the chances are they're going to spend some time rehearsing what they're going to say, so they can get their stories straight and have some ideas on how they are going to answer questions when they come up. Think about times you've lied or been tense going into a conversation, and you've planned in advance what you're going to say.

However, few people will rehearse their gestures and body language, which means that they can be dead giveaways to how people feel on the inside. This is why it's so important to keep an eye open for them!

Look for Signs of Stress

Now, there could be several reasons why someone shows signs of stress. You could be in a stressful situation, or that someone could be having a bad day. Showing signs of stress doesn't mean they're lying, but it can be an indication, so keep an eye out for it.

We've spoken about these signs a lot, but just for clarity, some of the other signs you can spot are a change in the skin or face color of the person. Usually, when people get stressed because they're lying, they can either go very pale or very red as the blood moves through their body at a changing rate.

What's more, Detective Darren Stanton also explains that people tend to rub the nerve on the back of their neck when they're stressed, so make sure you look out for this one! Off on a bit of a tangent here, but Stanton has carried out a lot of research when it comes to lying and found in his studies that people will lie over 200 times per day around the Christmas holiday because we're around our families and loved ones and "want to spare their feelings."

Interesting. A little saddening but interesting. Under the same point of being stressed, you can also look for coughs, stuttering, and pauses that indicate rising stress levels.

Listen for the No

As LaRae Quy explains, an official who has been a part of the FBI for over 25 years, she explains how the word no is very connected to when people are lying, and while innocent in itself, she explains how you should listen to how the word is being said because this is where you'll hear the giveaways you're being lied to. Some of the changes you'll need to look out for include:

- Saying no and looking in another direction (lack of eye contact)

- Saying no and actually closing their eyes

- Say "Noooooo" and stretching the word

- Saying the word no in a singsong way

You Could Be Wrong

Finally, I need to share this point because it could well and truly happen to you, and that is that even if you're convinced that someone is lying to you and they won't admit it, well, you could be wrong, and the other person could well be telling you the truth.

I'm going to talk about this a lot more in our eighth and final chapter, but the truth is, you could be blinded by some feeling, thought, or emotion that is convincing you that the other person is lying. You can't just decide someone is guilty for their lies when you don't have the hard facts, which is what this process is all about. However, if you get to the end of the process and the signs don't add up and state that someone is lying, the chances are that they're probably not lying.

If the signs tell you that the person isn't lying, and you go through the BASIC process, and it still says the person isn't lying, then you can't just forget everything and say they are. That's an unethical, uncompassionate way to live your life. Even if you hate the person you're dealing with, and you want them to be a liar more than anything, you simply can't just force your narrative into reality. Life doesn't work that way.

Be the emotionally intelligent person you are and apologize for accusing someone if you got it wrong. Mistakes happen to everybody. You just need to be adult enough to own yours.

Tips for Dealing with Different People in Your Life

For the remainder of this chapter, I want to focus on how you can deal with situations where you think you may be dealing with a liar or are in need of finding out the truth in the various groups that you'll interact with throughout your life. Of course, you'll speak to your partner differently than you would your colleague, so it's important for you to know how to deal with everyone individually.

I'm also going to share some facts about each group so you have a greater understanding of what kind of lies you can expect and what you're dealing with. However, I highly recommend reading through every section because there's some amazing information and techniques I've split up into each section that can overlap when dealing with different groups of people in your life.

Dealing with Men & Women

Men and women tend to lie in different ways and for various unique motives, so it's a good idea to understand both so you can deal with potential lies in any given situation. Let's start with the men.

The most common motive for men to lie is to boost their image of themselves. Think about situations like men trying to appear more interesting or successful than they actually are to impress someone they find attractive, to obtain a job position, or exaggerating the truth on their dating profile. In fact, statistics back this up by detailing that men tend to lie around eight times more often about themselves and their own lives than they tell lies about other people.

Although men and women seem to lie about the same number of times per day to the same frequency, the most common lies women tell are usually with the motive of either protecting the privacy or feelings of someone else in their life or to make them feel better about themselves.

So, how can you use this information? Well, it depends on whether you are a man or a woman. Multiple published research papers show that women tend to feel more guilty about their lies than men do and can even become anxious and fearful that their lies will be found out.

This means if you're talking to a woman and you suspect them of lying to you, then you may want to use some of the techniques we spoke about in the previous chapters to press and find out the truth. Research shows they are more likely to admit deceit if you focus on the lie for longer than usual.

However, figuring out whether someone is lying in the first place may be trickier if you're a man. Research shows that women are far more capable of detecting lies in other women, especially when they know them. The closer women are as friends to each other, the easier they can tell if they're lying or not, especially when compared to male friends who know each other to the same degree.

So, in a nutshell?

If you're a woman, the chances are you'll be able to detect lies better in your friends and the people you've known for a long time, so use the skills learned in the previous chapters and rely on your gut instinct to figure out whether someone is lying to you.

As a man, you'll need to pay extra attention to those who you think are lying to you, especially when communicating with other men since they'll typically be able to hide their lies from you without fear or anxiety holding them back.

Whenever you're conversing with either a man or a woman, look for lies in various situations. As above, women tend to lie most when protecting others or making themselves feel better. Some examples include:

- Protecting a friend in a friendship drama

- Not saying how someone else feels about another person

- Playing down a sad or irritating situation

- Saying everything is alright when it isn't

- Not telling the truth about a situation involving a partner, friend, or family member

In the same vein, men will lie to raise themselves up, so whenever you're in a situation where this could possibly occur, keep your eyes open for the signs. There are plenty of situations in your life when this can happen. For example:

- On a dating profile

- On a resume or CV

- When dating someone

- When applying for a job

- When talking about how well they performed at work

- Talking about how well a sports game or competition went

- Talking about past or present achievements

Dealing with Your Partner

It should go without saying that people who lie in their relationships with their partners end up having bad relationships. Any kind of romantic relationship is founded on the concept of trust, and without being able to fully trust your partner, you just know it's going to end badly.

Put it this way. Studies show that people in same-sex relationships (there's not much peer-reviewed data currently on other types of relationships) tend to have stronger, more responsible relationships with their other halves. Basically, you have better relationships with your partners when you don't lie to them. Each person who's truthful will be far more capable and responsible in the way they live their day-to-day lives. Perhaps not too shocking.

However, statistics show that lying does still occur. An incredible 85% of people in couples at a college-age will lie to their partner about the details of their past relationships, and around 10% of all married interactions contain some form of lie. That's still a relatively high figure, but when you consider that people tend to lie in every one in three interactions with people who aren't their spouses, sure, we lie less often to those we love, but when we do, they tend to be the biggest, most impactful lies of them all.

So, how do you deal with lying in your relationships?

First, when you're faced with a lie, determine its impact and severity. Has your partner told you a little white lie or a blatant, flat-out lie? You might say to yourself that a lie is a lie, and as we spoke about in recent chapters, even a small lie can have massive consequences, even more so when it comes from the person you're supposed to love and trust.

However, how you deal with the lie will depend on how it affects you in this way. Remember, you need to ask yourself these three questions:

- How much damage does the lie create?

- How long will the effects of the lie last?

- How is the relationship of the involved people affected by the lie?

For example, has your partner told you a lie because they want to avoid an argument about taking out the trash? Or are they lying about cheating on you with someone at work? If your partner is lying to you about everything being okay because really they're stressed out and don't want to look weak in front of you, then this is also a different story.

You need to judge a lie based on how you feel about it, the motive behind it, and the consequences it will have. Using the latter example about being stressed and not wanting to seem weak, if you recognize this lie, then you can say that it's okay to feel stressed, and it's even more okay to talk about. You may say that your partner doesn't need to push down how they feel and can feel open and comfortable talking about anything and everything with you. You can assure them there's certainly no reason to lie to you.

On the other hand, if your partner is lying to you about having an affair, then you may want to kick them out before they even know what's coming. The choice is up to you. Now, I know what you're thinking. Obviously, relationships are complicated, and a lot of things that occur in them are easier said than done. Sometimes, you're going to need to deal with lies in various ways depending on all manner of variables, such as the situation, the context, how you feel, how your day has been, what mindset you're both in, and so on.

So, how do you deal with it?

Well, at the end of the day, your partner is lying to you for one of two reasons. They're either lying to:

- Stop a fight or hard conversation from happening, or

- They are messing with your head

Both are pretty messed up in their own way. Ask yourself why your partner feels the need to lie. In some cases, they may be lying because they've tried having a conversation with you before, but your own judgments and criticisms made your partner feel unheard and unrespected, which means they don't want to bring it up again, nor talk to you about it.

I had two friends that dated for a short period of time, one of which suffered from severe depression. Their partner thought it was just him acting silly and that he should "buck up and man up," and this lack of respect about how it felt made him never want to talk to her about his illness. He just shoved it down and constantly lied that everything was okay all the time and would obviously project his negative feelings in other ways that ended up pushing them both apart.

However, when it comes down to it, the only way to address or stop lying from happening in your relationship is to be prepared to face the truth. This means you need to be open and accepting of the truth, no matter what it is, and actually have the ability to talk about the subject you're being lied to about. There'll be a reason you're being lied to, and this is a reason you'll need to come to terms with if you want honesty.

You may not like the answers, but this is just something you'll need to overcome.

Dealing with Your Parents

This is a tricky one. If your parents are lying to you, it can be a devastating realization and one that leaves you feeling a little weird. Of course, most parents lie to their children all the time, whether it's about Santa or the Tooth Fairy, but most of these lies are commonplace and are accepted by children later in life. After all, a fictional story is technically a lie and a falsehood but is entirely acceptable and valid in the right situations.

However, parents lying to their children from a young age about a lot of things can be catastrophic for the child's development. Parents need to encourage their children to sense and engage with their own internal sense of what's right or wrong. That goes back to what we've spoken about regarding gut instinct. However, if parents lie and manipulate their children into making sure they only follow what the parents say, children won't trust their own sense of judgment, which will lead to them having little to no self-dependence as they grow into adults.

People need to be able to trust themselves for their own self-confidence and self-esteem, but obviously, from a young age, there's very little you can do because you don't know a lot about the world. So, what happens when you grow up and realize your parents have been lying?

First, take note of what your parents have been lying about and what their motives for lying are. Here are some ideas of common things parents lie about:

- Parents saying they still love each other for the sake of the children when they don't.

- Being selfish and missing an important event but lying and saying they were busy or held up.

- Telling their children that everything is fine in the household when it's not.

- Making selfish decisions for the child and saying it's "in their best interest."

- Providing comfort in situations just to make the child happy.

- Ignoring a child's cry for help when they're older (such as a drug or drinking problem).

- Telling their children that their feelings aren't real—"You're not hurt!" when, in fact, they are.

- Lying about the impacts of negative events.

- Lying about big life events, like being sick or losing a job.

Of course, we can understand why parents do this. It's to protect their child from the truth, but this is so problematic in so many ways. Telling a child that they're okay when they fall over and hurt themselves invalidates how they're feeling, meaning they won't trust themselves and their own instincts when they're adults because they were told as children that how they felt wasn't real.

This affects so many people as adults. So, let's say you've grown up and faced some of these issues yourself. You realize your parents lied to you in the past and still lie to you from time to time now. This was commonplace in my own household while growing up. My parents were reasonably honest people, but my grandparents on my mother's side would lie endlessly about everything and anything they could, usually with the aim of making themselves look better in the eyes of others or attempting to get sympathy.

Unfortunately, you only have a few choices:

- Talk to your parents, call them up on their behavior, and have a hard conversation.

- Let the lying slip past, and just be mindful that it takes place, and you'll need to be aware of it.

- Sever ties in the relationship.

I wouldn't recommend the latter option unless you're living in an extreme situation where your parents are highly manipulative, and even still, I would always recommend having the hard conversation first. This means talking to your parents, pulling them up on lies they've told you, and questioning why this has been the case. You may even want to involve a family therapist or counselor who can help guide you through the process while keeping everything on track.

It is, admittedly, hard dealing with lying parents because there's always the level that a lot of parents have where they're older, wiser, and deserve more respect from their children, but this is a dated concept that many lying parents will simply use to justify their "I know best" behavior, and it's wrong. You shouldn't have to live your life in that way, and it's not normal.

Of course, most change becomes harder the older someone gets. My grandmother on my mother's side is over 95 years old, so we've decided there's really no point in having the hard conversation. It would be nice to inspire change, but she's a 95-year-old woman. We've decided just to let her enjoy her final years and make her smile. That's all. If you have a younger parent, it's up to you whether you want to approach them or not.

Dealing with Your Boss

Let's say you've gone to work, and for whatever reason, you've just found out your boss has lied to you about something. Whether it's over a project, over company policy, over your paycheck, or just something you've been working on, you've found out and detected a lie, and now you're wondering what to do about it.

The workplace is a place in our lives that is rife with liars. According to the statistics, there are so many lies that take place and that people even find acceptable—ranging from 58% of workers who believe lying to make a coworker feel better is fine to 30% who think it's okay to lie to a customer to make sure they're happy or are basically dealt with as quickly as possible.

With over half of all UK employees believing it's acceptable to lie to the company and about how much they enjoy working there, to the employer, other employees, and so on, it shouldn't be surprising that bosses lie to their staff. After all, you've probably experienced it yourself where a boss has told you something to make you work faster or to convince you to stay on longer hours.

You may have been told a shorter deadline in order to get something finished faster, or you may have even been promised extra vacation time if you work extra hours over the busier periods—a promise your boss had absolutely no interest in fulfilling. Maybe they lied about sorting out an interpersonal matter between you and another coworker and said they had raised the issue to HR when they simply didn't bother.

There are endless reasons as to why a boss could lie to you, but there's no reason why they should. Since you spent most of your life at work, it's important you can trust the people you're surrounding yourself with, especially those who are supposed to be in charge and lead the team. If you can't trust your own leaders, then there's no hope for real, genuine, meaningful success in the long term.

So, what can you do about it? Fortunately, there's a process you can go through that will help guide your actions and the way you can act while dealing with a lying boss. Of course, as with all the processes we've spoken about in this book, you can customize the process to suit you and your individual situation. If your boss is a compulsive, malicious, and manipulative liar, then you may need to seriously think about quitting your job and finding a new one without giving them the time of day. It's not always your place to fix things, but instead, you need to think about yourself and your own well-being.

Anyway, let's get into the process.

Step One: Ignore It

If your boss is lying to you or others to make themselves seem bigger, more successful, or more interesting than they actually are, then you could probably note this as just an ego power-hungry problem your manager has, and while pretty unfortunate, it's pretty commonplace in workplaces.

I used to work part-time in a cardboard-box printing factory, a huge manufacturing company, and any time the area manager came to visit, the boss would always be bragging about all the fantastic things he's done on the factory floor since the last visit when as workers, we knew that nothing had changed in the way we worked— not to the degree that he told his manager they had, anyway.

In situations like this, the impact of the lie is fairly minimal, and you could probably continue to live your life normally if you just ignored it. You can note that your boss tends to lie, so bear that in mind when you're speaking to them, but otherwise, you can stamp yourself as being non-affected.

Lots of people like to believe that life is a black-and-white picture. Either you trust someone with all your heart and soul, or they lie, and that trust is gone forever. Life is far more complicated than that, and there are endless grey areas, so yes, you may lose trust in someone, but it can take time to build it back up. While you'd probably be more hurt if your partner lied to you, there are always workarounds.

Bear in mind that your boss may have actually lied to you because they had positive intentions. They may have lied to motivate the team into believing they could do something and finish a project when they couldn't before (perhaps through the medium of telling a story about a team that pulled out all the stops to succeed). In this case, the lie was actually a good thing, so surely you'd be able to work around it.

Step Two - Addressing the Lie

While you may try and ignore or work around the lies your boss is saying, there may be times when you simply can't move on from the situation until the lie is addressed, which means you need to go and have a talk with them. This can be scary, especially when many employees will look at their bosses as figures of authority and status. You don't want to pull your boss up for them to then give you a hard time for the rest of your working life.

I'll start with this. Your boss is only a human being, just like you. They are not better people than you, nor worse people than you. You are both equals. Sure, them being your boss means that they could, in theory, make your working life a living hell, but then if this is the case, you need to ask yourself whether you actually want to work in a company where this kind of management style is deemed acceptable, and if your answer is no, then it's time to leave and work someone else. Literally, your own mental health and well-being depend on it.

So, how do you do it?

First, schedule a proper time to talk to your boss. Don't just catch them in the corridor and try to lay it on there and then, nor try and embarrass them by pulling them up in front of everyone else. Remember, this will only make them defensive and aggressive, which won't lead to a productive conversation. Go through the proper channels to organize a meeting to talk with them.

When you're sitting together, be frank and earnest with them. Try to leave out as much emotion from the conversation as possible and just state the hard facts in a way that is both clear and concise. Remember the tips we've spoken about in the previous chapters. You don't want to accuse your boss of lying because your information could be distorted. You could say something like:

"Thanks for your time. I wanted to talk to you because I heard you say that all the health and safety requirements have been met when I know for a fact they haven't, and it's putting us workers at risk."

If you go in with the hard and fast statements like:

"Hey. So you said that all the health and safety requirements had been met, and they're obviously not. What gives?"

See the difference? One leads to a productive conversation, whereas the other says, "You've done something wrong and lied, and now you're facing the consequences."

Again, you need to remember the techniques from the previous chapters. Don't go into the conversations with expectations and accusations. You may have your suspicions but allow your boss to explain why they said what they said so you could learn the whole picture before making a decision about what to do next.

Dealing with Your Coworkers

There's no doubt that having to deal with a coworker who is lying to you and everyone else is one of the most infuriating things to experience on the planet. In most jobs, we spend more of our awake time with our colleagues than we do with our own partners and family, and when those people are deceitful and dishonest, of course, it's going to leave a bitter taste in your mouth.

What's more, you've been very lucky if you've gone through your working life without a coworker lying to you. The workplace is one of the most common places for lies to be told, and following Pareto's Principle, around 20% of the people at work will tell 80% of the lies. As you read this, you're probably thinking about your workplace, and you know exactly who this section is referring to.

That person who always exaggerates how amazing their weekend was or how amazing the boss praised them for working so hard in their most recent performance meeting. They boast about how much the client or customers loved them or lie about getting loads of work done on the project when they really haven't done anything at all, and as always, they plan to leave their share of the work to be done at the last minute.

Perhaps the coworkers in your workplace are even more malicious than this. Maybe they're the kinds of people who spread rumors and gossip about other people at work around the office or will actively start drama between other coworkers. Perhaps they seem to thrive off this kind of chaos. Whatever you're dealing with, there's no doubt it's a lot, and it's taxing on your own peaceful state of mind, but this doesn't have to be the case when you know how to deal with it.

However, there are multiple ways you can deal with a liar at work, depending on who they are and what kind of liar they identify as.

Frequent Liars

Frequent liars are people who do not see that lying is a problem and therefore lie all the time. They're the kind of people who lie about everything and anything (usually compulsively). These liars, however, will most commonly lie when they're under pressure from others or a certain task. They will lie to get others off their back or to make the circumstances of a situation appear to be better than they really are (i.e., everything on the project is fine when it's actually not).

Some frequent liars will also lie to make it seem as though they're in control of a situation or lie to make themselves feel good or appear good in the eyes of others. However, what's interesting to note is that a 2013 study, "Being Honest About Dishonesty: Correlating Self-Reports and Actual Lying," found that frequent liars are far more likely to accept and own up to their lies because they really don't see anything unethically wrong with the act of lying.

Now, what's interesting about frequent liars is that they

are incredibly smart and usually have a lot of creative energy and brainpower. After all, to tell one lie usually means having to create ten other lies to justify the first, and so being able to get away with this is incredibly taxing on the mind. When dealing with a frequent liar, you mustn't be just trying to figure out the truth all the time but rather trying to find the truth when it matters most.

It's a bit sad that some people will have grown up in this way and learned that lying is the best way for some people to get what they want, but this is just the world we live in. So, if a frequent liar says that they enjoy working with you, this could be a lie. They might actually hate working with you, but if they continue to act as though they enjoy working with you and it doesn't cause any problems, then does it really matter if you find out the truth?

On the other hand, if the person lies about being able to finish their assigned project by the end of the week or declares they are university-educated, qualified, and know precisely what they're doing on this computer software, this could be a devastating lie because the chances are they'll be found out, and it will ruin their reputation. It's simply a lie not worth creating. However, that usually doesn't stop some people from trying, so when you suspect someone is lying in a way that matters, all you need to do is call them out on it as soon as you can, not allowing time and space for the lie to manifest and the other supporting lies to be created.

You may feel an urge to punish the liar for lying in the first place, but note that highlighting and recognizing when someone is lying can be more than enough of a punishment in itself for the liar, so just watch that space to ensure they don't continue.

Systematic Liars

As the name suggests, systematic liars are dishonest people who always seem to operate on a set kind of behavioral pattern, which makes them very easy to identify once you've found out and highlighted what they do and how they work. Consider how you may have that one friend who's always late, and it doesn't matter what the occasion is or what's going on; they can never seem to turn up on time. It's the same logic that applies here.

There are multiple reasons and triggers that can cause a systematic liar to lie. Maybe they're an unorganized person and are always running late on their deadlines. This means they're always making up excuses and lying as to why their work is late. Perhaps they feel insecure that their work isn't good enough and are plagued by self-doubt.

They could be the sort of person to get jealous easily, or like winding people up just for the fun of it, or perhaps even like getting attention from coworkers of the opposite sex. Whatever it is, all you need to do is look for the patterns in this person's behavior and then gently remind them that they don't need to lie. There's usually no need to punish this person; just a little eye-opening nudge every now and then can be enough to remind them of what they're doing.

Spontaneous Liars

These kinds of liars are the people who don't usually lie, but you may catch them in the act every now and then. These are basically the people who are the opposite of frequent and compulsive liars and will only be telling lies in the first place because they feel as though they've been driven to.

Your goal here is to identify the motive of the liar. Have they been triggered by an insecurity (which is usually the common reason), or are they trying to protect their ego and reputation, or the reputation of someone they care about? These could be small lies, like someone saying they've seen the recent Marvel movie when they actually haven't because they don't want to feel left out, or they have heard of the topic of conversation when they really haven't because they don't want to come across as stupid.

Instead of punishing and embarrassing these people, realize they're lying because they feel insecure about themselves. This is something you can alleviate by being kind, empathetic, and compassionate, and gently suggesting they don't need to lie and it's okay not to know everything or to feel bad about certain things. It's this approach that will encourage this person not to lie in the future.

Insecure Liars

Hand in hand with the lying type above, insecure liars are the predictable people who will lie about anything and everything when triggered. Insecure liars lie to make themselves feel better about themselves, to protect their egos, their reputations, and to make themselves seem better, smarter, or more capable in the eyes of others.

As with all these lying tips, insecure liars tend to lie when triggered, which means you can observe them over periods of time to determine what they're insecure about and, therefore, what triggers their dishonest behavior. In most cases, you'll only need to catch them lying once to clearly identify what their motive for lying is. Some examples of this could be exaggerating how well they did at a certain project or dealing with a certain client, or saying how well they performed in a meeting or performance review.

The best way to deal with these people is to remind them that they're okay just the way they are, and it doesn't matter if they're not the best at everything. They have value as the individual they are and don't need to exaggerate or pretend to be something they're not. They're still valuable as individuals. It's this kind of nurturing and validating response that will slowly allow them to be peaceful and not feel the need to lie in the future.

Dealing with Your Friends

It can be very difficult to deal with a friend who you've found out has been lying to you. You might feel as though you misplaced your trust massively, and it can hurt a lot. However, much like the other lying advice given in this chapter, there are plenty of ways to go about it.

First, decide on the severity and impact of the lie. Did they lie to make you feel better? Did they lie because they're struggling with their own problems and are feeling trapped but don't want to admit it? Did they lie to protect themselves or something else? Did their lie have positive intentions? Did they lie to maliciously hurt you?

It's so important you take the time to answer these questions to decide how you respond. And remember, dealing with a friend who's lied to you is going to make you feel emotional, so take a moment to sit back and allow your feelings and emotions to settle so you can be grounded. If you head into a conversation to confront your friend when you're hurt, and you have your guns blazing, it's not going to be a productive conversation.

When you do confront your friend with their lie, use the techniques we've spoken about up to this point. Are they lying because they feel insecure? Does your friend even know they are lying? Do they know the whole story?

Have an honest, deliberate, and intentional conversation with your friend, and then decide what you want to do. You may want to forgive them and rebuild your trust. If the impact of the lie was small, perhaps it's something you can quickly move on from. In severe cases, you may want to reevaluate whether you want to remain friends with this person you thought you could trust.

It all starts with having the conversation where you're able to address the issues, find out the truth, collect the facts, and then allow yourself to make a grounded decision on what to do next. Just don't jump to conclusions or make assumptions before you know what's going on.

Dealing with Strangers

Finally, we come to the point of strangers who are lying to you. This is a bit of a broad one because it could be anyone, anywhere. Maybe the person in the shop lied about having a product not in stock because they couldn't be bothered to go out back and look for it. Maybe someone gave you false information because they thought it would be funny. It could be anything.

However, how you deal with these liars is entirely up to you. You could take it personally, cause a big scene, call that person out on their lie, and confront them, but you need to ask yourself whether it's really worth it. It's all well and good taking things to heart and feeling betrayed by someone you don't really know, but let's get real: it's probably not worth investing that much time and energy into. It's not worth allowing yourself to get stressed out and upset over something someone said who you're never going to see again. In this case, it can really be best to just let it go.

If someone lies, you may feel the need to confront them, but again, is it really worth the stress? There is the saying that there are two types of evil. Some people do evil things, and then some people see evil things happening and do nothing about it. You may feel the urge to take it upon yourself to try and "fix" the other person and show them the error of their ways, but this can be so risky.

A lot of people will simply shut down when confronted, especially when it's a confrontation by a stranger they don't know who's telling them that their decisions on how to live their life are wrong. Sure, you may get through to them in the long run. They may go home and think about what they've done, but the chances are they won't. You can't fix every problem in the world, just like you can't go around the city and give every homeless person a roof to sleep under. It's just not feasible, and in many cases, not a productive solution.

Learn when it's best to walk away and let it go, and this applies to all groups of people in your life, not just strangers.

With that, we come to the end of this chapter, and damn, that was a packed one! I hope you saw what I meant at the beginning when it came to how all the techniques and advice somewhat merge into one another. You can certainly use various techniques, strategies, and approaches with the people in your life. It's all about reading the situations and figuring out the best approach for the individual context you're dealing with.

And now we move on to our eighth and final chapter: obstacles. I've spoken a bit about some of the obstacles you'll face when reading, identifying, processing, and confronting a liar in your life, but now we're going to cover everything we've missed and tie up all the loose ends.

Chapter Eight - Obstacles That Blind You from the Truth

The truth hurts. The truth will set you free. All that matters is the truth. The truth is a strange thing. While the vast majority of people would agree that the truth is the best thing out there, and dishonesty is the worst, a lot of us do try to avoid the truth as much as we can, because yes, while the truth is good, it can be difficult to face. Sometimes we just don't want to know the truth, and sometimes it eludes us, even when we strive for it.

This is why we cry when we find out we've been living with serious medical problems. Or when a truth we knew deep-down turned out to be true, but now it's been consciously realized. Or we still buy clothes from companies that are known to manufacture their products in sweatshops. The truth is strange.

There are endless obstacles you could come across when trying to find out the truth with the situations and people in your life, and I'm going to address some of the most important in this chapter. This is important to know because it allows you to see the truth when you want to see it and will help you stop yourself from being clouded by judgments that could alter your perspective. Let's jump straight in.

You're in Love

Let's start with an easy one. If you're in love with someone, be it a friend, romantic partner, spouse, sibling, or parent, it's incredibly easy to be distracted when trying to find out the truth. If you've been lied to, it can hurt. You may not want to accept that someone you care about has been dishonest with you in the first place, and you may not want to find out the truth.

Let's say you've been cheated on. You want to know the truth because you want to know where you stand, what happens, and how your relationship is going to move forward, but finding out the cold hard truth and actually hearing that your loved one has betrayed you can be an incredibly hurtful thing to hear.

It's very important that when you're dealing with a loved one who's lied to you, you take all the time you need to actually address what's happened and to process any emotions you're feeling. It can be very tempting and relatively commonplace to have a conversation when you're feeling emotional. You may have a lot of resentment, anger, or sadness that you need to vent, and that's fine. Let it out.

However, before making any big life decisions, make sure you're taking some time out to breathe and process the situation. Allow your emotions to settle and your grounded, rational way of thinking to come into play. This is very important because if you're making emotionally driven decisions, you may end up saying or doing something you'll regret. Be patient.

What's more, make sure you're being mindful of what's being said to you. Some people may lie to you because they know you love them and that you'll believe what they're saying. While I'm not saying you need to be paranoid of everything anyone says to you and constantly on the lookout for lies, if you feel like you're being lied to by a loved one, then don't let these feelings go amiss by ignoring them. Just pay extra attention until you're sure you've found out the truth.

You're Emotional

Hand in hand with the point above, if you're feeling any kind of emotion, then this could inhibit your ability to see the lies of someone else or to stop you from seeing the truth. You could be feeling stressed, anxious, or exhausted from a busy day. You could be feeling panicky, sad, or even really happy. Even being in a very positive state of mind where everything in the world looks amazing can leave you in a position where you overlook when someone is telling you a lie because you're not looking for it or paying attention to body language and verbal signs of dishonesty.

Again, I'm not saying that you need to feel as though you should be paranoid and on the lookout for lies all the time. Of course, you can let your guard down and relax. If you're feeling stressed, you don't need to make things worse by constantly being on the lookout for lies. The point is that feeling this way does mean you could miss the signs, so just be wary of this when going into certain situations.

For example, if you're trying to have a serious conversation with your partner, but you're feeling anxious and stressed, then recognize this and decide whether you think it's best to continue or to step back and put the conversation on hold until you're feeling more grounded and balanced.

The Lies are Easy

Sometimes, it's easy to go along with a lie or to accept it because you don't want to have to deal with the truth. Whether at work or dealing with a lying friend, it can be easy to feel like dismissing the truth and just going along with the fiction someone else is creating. You may think,

Oh, it's only a little lie, so I won't waste my time addressing it, or you just don't care about the matter.

That's fine, but remember that lies have hidden impacts, and if someone is allowed to get away with a lie once, then the chances are they're going to lie again in the future. If you catch someone lying to someone else in a way that doesn't affect you, then bear in mind the same person may find it acceptable to lie to you or already has.

While it may be hard and even scary to confront a liar, and you may feel like there's no point, you're really going to deny yourself genuine satisfaction and fulfillment in life if you allow yourself to be surrounded by dishonesty.

The Truth is Hard & Uncomfortable

Simultaneously with the consideration above, the truth can be hard to deal with, and sometimes, you're just not going to want to know. I go back to the point of being cheated on by your partner. You may be hurt and sad because you have your suspicions that it's happening, but actually being told your suspicions are true is a whole other level of pain and hurt. Sometimes, you're just not going to want to face it.

However, you need to consider the alternative, especially in situations like this. Do you want to face the truth and understand what's going on in your life, or do you want to hide from it and live with someone who tells you lies? Sometimes, addressing something now means you can live free in the future.

You're Scared of Change

Coming to terms with a lie means that some aspect of your life is going to change. Something you once thought was part of your reality is now changing into something else, and as human beings, we're designed to see change as this big, scary thing that we believe we should shy away from because it's the unknown. The brain loves to live in a comfort zone.

However, this goes back to what we've already said about asking yourself how you want to live your life. Do you want to live in a false reality, or do you want to know what's going on so you're able to make decisions that are productive and beneficial to your life, not just based on stories? It's up to you.

Reputation or Ego Protection

Sometimes, learning the truth means learning about the views and opinions of others and how they see themselves, how they see the world, and how they see you, and this can be tough to deal with. Of course, as social creatures, we want other people to like us. We want to fit into our tribes and be valued members, and learning the truth that someone doesn't actually like you very much when you thought they did can be a bit unsettling.

However, you must see these truths for what they are and don't delude yourself with fiction. Again, this means addressing, acknowledging, and accepting how you feel in the short term to be better off in the long term. Trust me, as with all these points and obstacles, Future You will thank you in the long run!

As you can see, many obstacles can get in the way of you seeing the truth for what it really is, and there are going to be times you just don't want to know, whether you think it's going to hurt too much, you don't care to know, or it's going to make you feel insecure. If you find out that someone who's been in your life for a long time has been lying to you constantly, then, of course, one of the first things you're going to think is how you could have been so stupid and not seen the signs before.

But you're not stupid. You're not anything else than amazing. This is perhaps the reason why you picked up this book in the first place: to learn the skills needed to see reality for what it really is. To have the ability to see the truth. Life is all about learning one lesson after another and growing through every day, and every year you're on this planet—always evolving and ever-changing.

Every experience can be a lesson if you learn to see the world in this way, and dealing with dishonesty in your life is just another skill you can master.

Final Thoughts

With that last chapter, we now come to the end of this journey. I know, I know, it's been emotional, and there's been so much to take in. What I love about the process of writing these books is the journey of being able to deep-dive into a subject like this and learn everything there is to know. I'm sure we can all admit that we'd benefit from the ability to spot when someone else is telling a lie, but actually learning about the nuances and strategies on how to do it is such an incredible experience, and investing our time here helps teach us a skill that will surely last a lifetime.

It's an amazing thing, and I'm so glad we were able to share this journey together. Now it's over to you. Take your skills and your teachings and go put them into practice. It won't be something you can master overnight, but with a bit of mindfulness and slowly applying everything you've learned in this book into your day-to-day life, you'll start to see significant changes.

Give it time and see what happens! Be your own proof!

That's all from me for now. While you're here, I want to thank you for taking the time to read through this book. I hope you got a lot out of it. A quick little ask is that if you did enjoy this book, then be sure to head over to wherever you picked up your copy and leave me a review! I love hearing your feedback and your thoughts and experiences of reading my work. I'm on my own journey of doing what I love and finding my way, and I want to listen to what you have to say so I can become the best version of my writer self!

Any feedback is always appreciated! What's more, be sure to check out this series to see whether there are any other life lessons and self-development journeys you're interested in taking. It's been a busy few years for me, so there's certainly a lot to look through! Anyway, keep up the practice, and best of luck to you! Enjoy your journey!

See you soon!

Also by James W. Williams

- How to Read People Like a Book: A Guide to Speed-Reading People, Understand Body Language and Emotions, Decode Intentions, and Connect Effortlessly
- Communication Skills Training: How to Talk to Anyone, Connect Effortlessly, Develop Charisma, and Become a People Person
- How to Make People Laugh: Develop Confidence and Charisma, Master Improv Comedy, and Be More Witty with Anyone, Anytime, Anywhere
- Digital Minimalism in Everyday Life: Overcome Technology Addiction, Declutter Your Mind, and Reclaim Your Freedom
- Self-discipline Mastery: Develop Navy Seal Mental Toughness, Unbreakable Grit, Spartan Mindset, Build Good Habits, and Increase Your Productivity
- How to Make People Like You: 19 Science-Based Methods to Increase Your Charisma, Spark Attraction, Win Friends, and Connect Effortlessly
- How to Make People Do What You Want: Methods of Subtle Psychology to Read People, Persuade, and Influence Human Behavior

- How to Talk to Anyone About Anything: Improve Your Social Skills, Master Small Talk, Connect Effortlessly, and Make Real Friends
- Listening Skills Training: How to Truly Listen, Understand, and Validate for Better and Deeper Connections

References

Gaille, B. (2021). 25 Nose Growing Statistics on Lying. Retrieved 8 May 2021, from https://brandongaille.com/24-nose-growing-statistics-on-lying/

Why Do People Lie: 9 Motives for Telling Lies. (2021). Retrieved 8 May 2021, from https://www.paulekman.com/blog/why-do-people-lie-motives/

3 Considerations Impacting the Severity of a Lie. (2021). Retrieved 8 May 2021, from https://www.linkedin.com/pulse/3-considerations-impacting-severity-lie-jeff-aucoin

Margaret Banford, M. (2021). The Body Language of Lying: Top Secrets Revealed by Psychologists - Learning Mind. Retrieved 8 May 2021, from https://www.learning-mind.com/the-body-language-of-lying/

Science Says Using This Really Simple Trick Can Stop Someone From Lying To You. (2021). Retrieved 8 May 2021, from https://www.elitedaily.com/p/heres-how-to-get-the-truth-out-of-someone-using-a-simple-science-backed-trick-13153582

How to get someone to tell you the truth. (2021). Retrieved 8 May 2021, from https://www.psychologies.co.uk/how-get-someone-tell-you-truth

Valerie Soleil, L. (2021). The Psychology of Lying: What Happens When We Lie? [INFOGRAPHIC] - Learning Mind. Retrieved 8 May 2021, from https://www.learning-mind.com/the-psychology-of-lying-what-happens-when-we-lie-infographic/

Truth, 1., & Editor, B. (2021). 10 Reasons Why We Avoid Truth. Retrieved 8 May 2021, from https://www.beliefnet.com/wellness/galleries/10-reasons-why-we-avoid-truth.aspx

12 signs someone is lying to you. (2021). Retrieved 8 May 2021, from https://www.independent.co.uk/life-style/signs-someone-lying-not-telling-truth-a7606246.html

Houston, P., Floyd, M., Carnicero, S., & Tennant, D. *Spy the lie.*

6 Ways to Detect a Liar in Just Seconds. (2021). Retrieved 8 May 2021, from https://www.psychologytoday.com/gb/blog/hope-relationships/201507/6-ways-detect-liar-in-just-seconds

Meyer, P. *Liespotting*.

When Parents Lie. (2021). Retrieved 8 May 2021, from https://www.psychologytoday.com/us/blog/savvy-parenting/201406/when-parents-lie

Lies in the Workplace. (2021). Retrieved 8 May 2021, from https://www.psychologytoday.com/us/blog/the-nature-deception/201907/lies-in-the-workplace

How Often Do We Lie at Work? (2020, February 19). The Viking Blog. https://blog.viking-direct.co.uk/lying-at-work

Lastoe, S. (2016, February 23). *3 Ways to Deal With a Lying Co-worker (That Don't Involve Losing It)*. Themuse.com; The Muse. https://www.themuse.com/advice/3-ways-to-deal-with-a-lying-coworker-that-dont-involve-losing-it

Halevy, R., Shalvi, S., & Verschuere, B. (2013). Being Honest About Dishonesty: Correlating Self-Reports and Actual Lying. *Human Communication Research*, *40*(1), 54–72. https://doi.org/10.1111/hcre.12019

September 2009, J. B. 29. (n.d.). *Parents Lie to Children Surprisingly Often*. Livescience.com. Retrieved May 8, 2021, from http://www.livescience.com/culture/090929-parents-lie.html

How to Be a Better Listener | Psychology Today. (n.d.). Www.psychologytoday.com. Retrieved May 8, 2021, from https://www.psychologytoday.com/us/blog/lifes-work/202006/how-be-better-listener

Bagaric, M. (2007, February 8). *Is "glass ceiling" worth breaking?* The Age. http://www.theage.com.au/news/business/is-glass-ceiling-worth-breaking/2007/02/07/1170524164582.html

How To Sniff Out A Liar. (n.d.). Forbes. Retrieved May 8, 2021, from http://www.forbes.com/2009/05/13/lie-detector-madoff-entrepreneurs-sales-marketing-liar.htmlDePaulo et. al,

"Lying in Everyday Life" 989–990; also, Vrij, *Detecting Lies and Deceit*, 26–28; also, DePaulo, Jennifer D. Epstein, and Melissa M. Wyer, "Sex Differences in Lying: How Women and Men Deal with the Dilemma of Deceit," Lewis and Saarni *Lying and Deception*, 126–147.

Allison Komet, "The Truth About Lying," *Psychology Today*, May 1, 1997, http://www.psychologytoday.com/articles/199705/the-truth-about-lying?page=2.

May 2006, R. L. 15. (n.d.). *Why We Lie.* Livescience.com. Retrieved May 8, 2021, from

http://www.livescience.com/health/060515_why_lie.h
tml

Rosemary Haefner, "Outrageous Résumé Lies,"
CareerBuilder.com, August 2008

APA   PsycNet.   (n.d.).   Psycnet.apa.org.
https://psycnet.apa.org/fulltext/2016-46793-001.html

The Psychology of Mirroring. (2017, October 31).
Imagine   Health.   https://imaginehealth.ie/the-
psychology-of-mirroring/

Jalili, C. (2018, November 30). *How to Tell If Someone
Is Lying to You, According to Body Language Experts.*
Time; Time. https://time.com/5443204/signs-lying-
body-language-experts/